FINANCIAL FREEDOM BLUEPRINT

I0479093

HUSTLE UP

53 No to Low-Cost Side Gigs to Boost
Your Income

BY SHANNON ATKINSON

CONTENTS

INTRODUCTION

Many individuals seek other means of generating more income in the current economic scenario. Due to the difficulty of the current so-called "credit crunch," we would gladly accept some additional funds. In our technological age, many people resort to the internet for ideas and inspiration to make this happen.

The good news is that generating money on the internet is possible with effort and perseverance. If you have performed a Google search on how to make money online, you have likely encountered many advertisements claiming you will earn between $3,000 and $20,000 a week. This is not a lie, but getting such results will require time and effort.

Some advertisements are legitimate and provide training courses and e-books on how to make money online, while the majority are likely to be scams. Therefore, you cannot expect to purchase a $20 bundle and immediately earn $200,000 weekly. If you have invested your money wisely and are willing to spend a small amount ($10 to $60), you should produce an internet income.

You must ask yourself whether or not you can afford to spend a few months learning, reading, and even creating your website (which is quite simple these days) and giving it your all. If the answer is YES, then it isn't a fallacy that no one can make money online and that we are all skeptics.

So, if you have established a successful internet money-maker, consider the following: Will we go to dinner tonight? Yes, the greatest restaurant, please.

What automobile should I get - how about a Corvette?

No maxing out credit cards and borrowing to pay off bills.

If your hard work has paid off, you might even consider quitting your job; imagine waking up and finishing work whenever you please. Sweet!!

If you are determined, you could be in this position in a year.

Check out my recommendations for the greatest and most successful packages, and if you'd want to make extra cash on the side and don't take this quite so seriously, you may do so with my other suggestions.

Attempting to eliminate debt is difficult, significantly if your salary cannot sustain it in addition to your actual expenses. If there is no other method to reduce your expenditures, your only choice is to improve your existing cash flow.

Here is where the side hustle comes into play. It simply refers to whatever income you receive outside of your monthly salary. It is a fantastic strategy to grow your debt payment fund, allowing you to become debt-free much more quickly.

Having two income sources is one of the finest strategies to attain financial security. Even if you lose one source of income, you still have another to maintain yourself and your family.

Even though you are investigating this to assist pay off your obligations, you can continue doing so even when you no longer owe money. It will undoubtedly be useful in the future. Also, this is an excellent way to develop your emergency money. It is advisable to be ready for any situation.

This GUIDE offers suggestions that may prove helpful as you search for the most lucrative supplementary income. Note that these are activities you can engage in during your free time. Choose the one you are most enthusiastic about or one you can turn into a hobby. It is best to pursue a passion and make a living from it. Thus, it would not feel at all like work.

Let's get started

CHAPTER 1

WEBSITE FLIPPING

Website flipping has evolved as one of the internet's most successful enterprises. Undoubtedly, expert website flipping may provide astronomical profits with minimal or no initial investment.

There are two ways to enter the lucrative website-flipping industry:

1. Creating one's website: Creating one's website can save money on investments, as one can create a great website with solid content, purchase an impressive domain name, monetize the flip website to the appropriate level and find a buyer on one of the prominent auction platforms.

2. Purchase and renovate an existing website: It is a simpler and quicker approach to entering the firm but requires an investment.

Essential measures in gaining money through website flipping include the following:

1. Acquiring a decent domain name: A domain name that is concise and memorable while still conveying the essence of the website's content can go a long way for any business. Consequently, purchasing a decent domain name is crucial to enhancing the worth of your flip website.

2. Build or locate a template: The next essential step is to create or find a template that complements the identified niche. To ensure that all other pages are linked to the homepage, one must possess fundamental HTML knowledge. Adding free Photoshop templates to the flip

websites will give them a more professional appearance, significantly enhancing their value.

3. Monetize your flip website: Monetizing a flip website will attract high-paying buyers to your website. Potential purchasers actively seek monetized sites because it saves them considerable time and effort.

They only need to begin promoting the website via affiliate links. While monetizing your website, it is strongly advised that you solely explore Clickbank and AdSense items. In contrast to other websites, these two are highly lenient; hence, the consumer will not encounter any issues in the future.

4. Sell your flip website: Before selling your flip website, make sure you've taken all the essential procedures, such as boosting traffic and sales. One should also attempt to increase the website's ranking on search engines, as websites with higher rankings fetch a higher price. After ensuring that everything is flawless, you can sell the flip website on websites such as eBay, Digital Point, or Sitepoint.

CHAPTER 2

BAKING

Do you have magical hands when it comes to cooking and baking? Do you enjoy feeding your guests and witnessing their satisfied smiles? Then, the food industry is the perfect business opportunity for you!

The alternatives are so varied that one might spend a lifetime developing new recipes and locating new consumer bases.

One of the ideas is to operate a catering business from home. To determine the market's need, one can begin by catering to local offices on a limited basis. Often, smaller companies lack a cafeteria, making it difficult for employees to find even the most basic foods. Catering to such establishments benefits the employees and is lucrative for your business.

There is also the option to serve nearby houses. In most households today, both parents work. This leaves the ladies with no time to cook, so they typically rely on TV dinners or fast food. Providing healthy, well-balanced meals at cheap rates will do wonders for their health, and there will undoubtedly be a large client base for this type of concept.

It is highly beneficial to survey the neighborhood and determine the current demand. If you feel prepared to take on more responsibilities, you can even provide catering services for parties organized by others. Rather than ordering food from a restaurant, individuals will want to consume distinctive and wholesome home-cooked meals.

A fantastic idea is a few signature dishes to distinguish your brand in the marketplace. If you have a knack for baking, this is unquestionably the way to proceed. Cakes, cookies, cupcakes, and biscuits, you name it; if you have the necessary skills and recipes, you will undoubtedly be a successful entrepreneur.

A bake sale in your yard can be a fantastic way to get the ball moving or set up a booth at a neighborhood festival or one of your children's school carnivals. As a result, neighborhood neighbors will be aware of your talent, and you can distribute a few business cards describing your products.

One must remember to get preliminary licensing from the local health authority, which confirms the cleanliness of your kitchen and cooking conditions. This provides an added selling factor, as you can position yourself as a safe and healthy certified food source, which is unquestionably an added advantage.

If you lack the financial resources to purchase cooking equipment, you can also become a personal chef! You may travel to individuals' houses and provide a delectable meal for their parties or gatherings. Having a crew of one or two sous-chefs to divide the workload is also brilliant. So what are you waiting for? Put on your aprons and prepare a delectable lunch!

CHAPTER 3

PET SITTING

People are becoming increasingly aware that starting a pet-sitting business is a fantastic opportunity to earn money and run your own business. This is the right business for animal lovers. While their owners are gone, you will care for the pets, brush them, feed them and shower them with affection, hugs, and company.

You can provide security for their home while they are away by turning on and off lights, collecting mail and newspapers, and watering plants. Even though it is a pet service, you must also enjoy working with people. You may have decided to become a pet sitter because you have a passion for animals, but a basic understanding of business procedures would be beneficial.

Your Commitment to Time

Start with a business plan if you are considering starting your pet-sitting service. Determine just how much time you can devote to pet care. Add travel time to and from their houses. After determining this, you will be able to sell your services effectively. Do not accept more than you can reasonably manage.

Determine How Much To Charge

Next, determine if others in your region offer pet-sitting services and their rates. You should also inspect kennels to provide your clients with competitive pricing. Consider the distance you need to travel to pet sit. The distance is too far, and gas prices may be prohibitive.

Do you wish to increase prices on holidays? Consider that many pet caregivers charge extra costs during the holidays and pet sitters are in such high demand during the holidays that their availability is often booked months in advance.

Consider employing help during this hectic season to increase your profits. However, introduce your aides to the owners and pets before the appointed pet-sitting time. Get the owners' permission for your assistance in caring for their pets.

As your business grows, YOU pick how many hours per day, week and month you wish to work. The Pet Sitting Business Start-Up Kit includes instructions for estimating potential earnings.

Which Animals Will You Watch?

The second step is determining the pets you will care for in your pet-sitting service. Some individuals prefer working with little dogs and cats since they need less effort and time than larger animals.

Some pet sitters accept various kinds of animals, from hamsters to horses and fish, birds, mice, rabbits, and pigs. That is the beauty of owning your own business: you have the opportunity to choose exactly which dogs you choose to care for.

Currently, dog walking services are highly popular. You will exercise and feed the dogs during the owners' absence. Alternatively, you might open a doggie daycare in your own house. Owners leave their pets at your location to be supervised and exercised during the day. If you have a large yard, this is an excellent alternative.

Forms provide a record of your visit in writing.

Those who employ a pet-sitting service typically view their pets as children, and minor details mean greatly to them. It would be best if you supplied the pet owners with a daily written report detailing your pet care. The owner will then see that you exert extra effort and genuinely care for their family pets.

Leave a Welcome Back form to remind the owners to call you to let you know they have arrived; take extra precautions not to abandon a pet whose owner missed their journey home.

The pet-sitting industry is thriving. It benefits the company owner, the pet owner, and the animal. The company owner can pursue their passion, and the pet owner can travel for work or pleasure without worrying about their pets.

Announce Your Business

A well-written press release might be advantageous to your business. You can get free advertising for your new pet company by submitting it to local publications. Your local newspaper's editor may decide to publish a feature piece about you and your pet company after reading your press release.

CHAPTER 4

CRAFTS

It makes perfect sense to make money from crafts and hobbies in today's society. Everyone could use a few extra dollars to spend on rising gas prices or even groceries. Everything is affected by increased gas prices, so whatever we can do to save a little side hustle will be helpful.

Consider for a moment how you may benefit from your crafts and hobbies. I'll wager that you can create a unique item that no one in your area can build, or perhaps, your cookies are the greatest in town.

Are you willing to divulge a secret recipe?

My father began fiddling with discarded conduit tubing years ago. Using the pipe, some fishing line, and a piece of plastic, he created wind chimes with a unique sound. He hung some on the front porch and constructed a platform to hang others in the front yard.

Within hours, he had more people than he could handle banging on his door and asking how much he would charge for manufacturing one or two for them. Without a strategy, he had converted his hobby of tinkering into a way to earn money from arts and crafts.

You can perform the same action. My neighbor earns a substantial income by making jewelry from small rocks, beads, and the like. He sets up a small booth at local craft events and fairs and sells his handmade jewelry, like hot cakes.

Consider the matter carefully. What hobbies and interests might you employ to earn some extra cash? Quilting is an excellent illustration. Very few people understand the craft of quilting, but many people are willing to pay a fortune for a handmade quilt. It is pretty easy to create beautiful jewelry from a few beads. Homemade jewelry is a trendy item. If you put your mind to action, you will soon make more money than ever from crafts.

CHAPTER 5

PART-TIME TRUCKER

Trucking is one of those businesses that offer some full-time and part-time career options. In the same way that a part-time trucking job can help you decide if this is an excellent full-time vocation, this can be a good alternative for those searching for a secondary income. Before choosing trucking as a second work choice, there are some crucial factors to consider, possibly more so than in other industries.

The Training Aspect

If you do not already possess a CDL, your employment options in the trucking business will be restricted. You may get work unloading and loading trucks at terminals, docks, and enterprises as an assistant. However, you will not be driving; you will be riding along.

Driver training for a CDL will take at least three weeks of full-time study and much longer if completed in the evenings and on weekends. However, training is not equivalent to experience, and even with a CDL, you may not have the expertise that larger companies want for insurance and liability reasons. Local, smaller companies often only hire full-time drivers, but you may be able to join with an owner-operator to assist with long-distance journeys.

The Timing Aspect

When attempting to coordinate part-time trucking work with full-time or other part-time employment, timing will also be challenging. This is because many occupations in the business do not adhere to a typical nine-to-five timetable. Depending on the task's requirements, you could be loading at midnight or unloading at 2:00 in the afternoon.

Many trucking jobs demand you to arrive at a spot within a specific schedule, yet you may have to wait hours before you can access the dock or terminal to unload. Scheduling the drive is simple, but you cannot predict how long you will be at the destination waiting to unload.

Unforeseen complications, including vehicle breakdowns, weather-related road closures, and route modifications, may also make arranging work as a second job exceedingly tricky.

The Experience Aspect

Insurance for a full-time driver is a significant expense for an employer or owner-operator. Insurance premiums can be significantly higher with a part-time driver with limited experience, recently graduated from CDL driving school, and logged few miles. In addition, driving half-time may not provide a realistic representation of what it would be like to go full-time.

Part-time driving is a viable choice if you are an experienced driver considering a return to the trucking profession after a break. In this situation, you will have the experience and understanding of what you want to do and work part-time to gain entry into a freight company. This part-time employment is more likely to be seasonal or to fill in for absent regular drivers.

You can drive part-time if you are fortunate enough to discover the proper combination of present employment and trucking employer. Remember that trucking is a difficult job with long days and nights on the road, which may or may not complement your full-time job.

Take a week or two of vacation and make arrangements to ride with an owner-operator on a lengthy voyage. While you cannot drive, you will better understand the trucking industry as an OTR driver. Then, if you enjoy that time, look for a part-time position, complete the necessary training and prepare to begin a full-time trucking career.

CHAPTER 6

ERRAND SERVICES

An errand service is your greatest option if you seek a home-based business opportunity that can be launched quickly, cheaply, and profitably. You are a personal assistant for busy people on an errand, often a concierge service. You would be compensated for running their chores on their behalf.

These chores could be as easy as paying utility bills, picking up groceries, or doing the laundry, or as sophisticated as organizing and arranging vacations for customers, meeting and event preparation, senior care, etc.

In today's hectic society, even the most basic errands are impossible for working individuals to complete. Therefore, they continuously look for methods to use their time correctly to enjoy more important things in life. They would gladly pay someone to complete their errands, giving them peace of mind and more time to enjoy life.

This is one of the primary reasons why this service industry is rapidly becoming a multimillion-dollar enterprise. In addition to individuals who rely on errand services to run their usual errands due to their busy schedules, there is a unique subset of individuals who rely on errand services to run their routine errands.

They require assistance with errands because they cannot leave their homes due to a new baby, disability, disease, or old age. They would prefer to pay for a service to run their errands than bother their family members.

In addition to the two groups described above, you can offer your services to small business owners who would prefer to hire you and send their employees to perform menial jobs. Accounting firms, advertising agencies, and legal firms are businesses employing errand-running services.

To start a basic errand service business, no specific training is required. However, you must be an outgoing organized individual with excellent interpersonal abilities. Since you may be required to perform the same jobs repeatedly and to travel, you should be versatile and mobile.

You should be computer literate if you intend to undertake sophisticated jobs, as they may include internet research, online reservations, etc. You should also receive training from an established concierge/errand service provider to learn the trade's skills.

Due to the developing nature of this profession, there are few venues to acquire training. Therefore, if you can train under an established concierge/errand service provider, you should maximize that opportunity.

As previously stated, a service for running errands can be simply established with the minimum initial investment. If you intend to perform only modest chores, you can get started with just a cell phone and trustworthy transportation.

To get your firm off to a successful start, you will need a reliable computer, printer, internet connection, software for monitoring your accounts and clients, a landline with voice mail, a mobile phone, a fax machine, and office supplies. If your services entail transportation, you would need to provide a vehicle.

The legal criteria for launching your business may differ based on the state in which you reside. Therefore, I advise you to consult an expert to comprehend the precise legal requirements.

Also, you may need to visit the municipal clerk's office and your state's Department of Revenue for assistance with the necessary paperwork and licensing before establishing your firm. Getting business insurance is a further worthwhile activity. Due to the high level of liability inherent in running an errand service business, this is incredibly useful.

As a provider of errand services, you would charge your clients by the hour or by the sort of service rendered. If you have recurring customers that use your services regularly, you can give them membership in exchange for an annual subscription covering a specified amount of monthly requests.

No matter how little your firm is at the outset, it is always recommended to develop a business plan. This will allow you to maintain a constant focus on your services while also managing the expansion of your organization. Marketing your services, essential for drawing customers, is another important activity you must perform.

This should be performed at the start of your firm and continuously. Networking is a cost-effective and inexpensive method for promoting your business. Also, you may use flyers, posters, brochures, emails, and sales letters to spread the news. Advertising via local newspapers, periodicals and trade publications or getting a listing in the Yellow Pages is a different method for attracting customers.

A website for your business is another excellent method of advertising your services. Always check that the information on your website is current and that you have included all your contact information.

CHAPTER 7

JANITORIAL SERVICES

Making money in the janitorial sector is crucial to the profitability of a janitorial business. There are some critical steps you must take to guarantee your financial success. Making money with your janitorial service is not as difficult as some believe, but it will demand your hard work, time, and patience.

Here are the most crucial steps you must take to ensure that your janitorial business will be profitable quickly.

1. You must ensure that the service you provide is reasonably priced. Customers prefer not to be concerned with any aspect of keeping their company clean. Ensure that your cleaning services cover all necessary cleaning tasks. This will aid in ensuring that your client is satisfied with your job and remains a client. They seek value, just as they would with any other company.

2. Promote your cleaning business. No one will ever learn that your business exists if you do not market it. You should utilize every method available to assist with marketing. Use flyers, business cards, a website, the local yellow pages, classified advertisements, and any other marketing strategy to attract new customers to your cleaning service.

3. Be careful not to accept too many clients at once. You want exceptional services, but this might be challenging if there are too many customers. It is usually preferable to have ten lucrative contracts for your janitorial service instead of 15 that are difficult to maintain.

4. Ensure familiarity with the cleaning sector. When attempting to earn money through cleaning services, it is essential to comprehend the market. Know about bidding and estimating, understand what your competitors are doing, and closely watch industry-specific developments.

By being informed of current events, it will be simple for you to earn money. Join one or more Janitorial Associations to stay abreast of changes in the cleaning business.

These are the most crucial tasks that must be completed for your janitorial service to generate revenue. By adhering strictly to these steps, you will ensure that your clients are constantly satisfied and that your business is always profitable. Combining all these actions is the best approach to ensure a lucrative janitorial business, so don't delay implementing them.

CHAPTER 8

FRANCHISE

If you've ever eaten at a terrific restaurant while on vacation and wished there was one in your hometown, perhaps you can purchase a franchise and open your own! Many entrepreneurs have created profitable businesses by utilizing the franchising market.

A franchise is a firm that authorizes an individual or group of individuals to engage in specified commercial activities. Franchising is a retail strategy employed to capture and maintain market share. This business strategy assists in creating a picture of the company's products and services in the minds of potential and present clients.

Franchising enables the dissemination of a tested business model, brand recognition development, and distribution and marketing assistance. Fundamentally, franchising entails a strategic alliance of persons with specific roles and responsibilities and a shared goal to conquer and control markets.

Essentially, purchasing a franchise entails investing in a tested business concept. You and the other franchisees must acquire and retain customers. You are required by law to serve customers utilizing the franchisor's operating and marketing systems.

Understand the legal ramifications of your relationship with other franchisees and the franchisor to be successful in franchising. You must realize that other franchisees are not your competition but mutually valuable assets for increasing brand awareness.

Listed below are some of the best franchises to consider. They are graded according to their original investment, growth, and eventual closure.

1. 7-Eleven

Joe C. Thompson, a former employee of the Southland Ice Company, created this company in 1927 and began selling bread, eggs, and milk in addition to ice blocks. He ultimately acquired the company and began opening convenience stores.

7-Eleven offers a renewable 10-year franchise deal with a customizable royalty rate. Franchise fees range from $10,000 to $1,000,000, while the total investment ranges from $30,000 to $1,600,000.

2. Subway

This business was founded in 1965 by Fred DeLuca and his friend Peter Buck in Connecticut with the express intention of funding DeLuca's college education. The company began franchising in 1974 and is today active in 98 countries worldwide.

The franchise agreement is renewable and lasts for twenty years. The recurring royalty charge for Subway franchisees is eight percent, and the initial investment ranges from $85,000 to $253,000.

3. Dunkin' Donuts

This company was founded in a Massachusetts doughnut shop. It is present in over 32 countries worldwide. They provide more than seventy varieties of donuts. This corporation collects a five percent royalty charge from franchisees. The agreement term is not renewed. To own such a franchise, you must invest between $300,000 and $1.5 million.

4. Pizza Hut

The franchise was established one year after being founded by Frank and Dan Carney in 1958. After more than fifty years, Pizza Hut may be found in many locations worldwide. Franchisees must pay a six percent recurring royalty fee and a $25,000 franchise fee throughout a twenty-year contract. The individual must have a minimum net worth of $700,000 and at least $350,000 in liquid assets.

5. Servpro

Ted and Doris Isaacson, the company's founders, converted their 1967-established painting business into a cleaning and restoration enterprise. This organization provides catastrophe restoration services, including cleanup and repairs after water or fire damage.

Prospective franchisees must have at least $100,000 in liquid assets and $85,000 in net worth. The franchise price is $43,000, and the royalty fee ranges from 3 to 10%. Investment totals range from $130,000 and $180,000.

To make money with a franchise, you should explore these leading candidates and research other firms that provide prospects. The franchise business is an excellent method to earn a living by delivering superior products and services to the community.

CHAPTER 9

A WEBSITE WITHOUT SELLING

U tilizing a website to earn money online has been one of the most prevalent methods in the modern era. There are some ways to make money with a website:

a) Sell only your goods and services.

b) Sell the goods of others (affiliate program).

c) Place Google advertisements on your website and earn money whenever an ad is clicked.

The first and second methods are time-intensive and demand Internet marketing expertise and experience. The third option to make money online is considerably more straightforward and quicker.

You must first sign up for the Google AdSense program to post Google advertisements on your website. You do not need a professional appearance or a fantastic website to join the Google AdSense program. A clean and straightforward website would suffice.

You can write about a topic or subject related to your experience, area of expertise, interests, or background for your website. If you are a specialist in a specific field, you can make your content relevant and beneficial to others by offering advice and instructional materials. If sports vehicles are your interest and hobby, you may introduce the newest models of sports cars and discuss the best tools for making them.

Even if you have no idea what to write about or have no interest in writing, you can still own an AdSense-generating website. Create a website dedicated to publishing articles authored by diverse authors. Simply select one or more topics, place multiple relevant articles per topic, then add Google advertising on each article page.

Create an AdSense website with minimal expense

It is costly to hire a professional to create a website. Finding a freelance web designer will be far less expensive. However, hiring a freelancer is not the most effective strategy to save expenses. Utilizing a free website builder to develop a website is the most cost-effective method of minimizing costs.

Many free website builders enable people to create websites without experience or technical expertise. You may locate these simple site builders using major search engines such as Google and Yahoo. With a site builder, you can have one or many free websites. You solely pay for the website's domain name and hosting.

Once your website has been launched, you must determine how to attract people to your website. Your website cannot produce revenue if nobody views it. There are many strategies to attract targeted visitors to your website quickly.

PPC (pay-per-click) campaigns

Pay-per-click (PPC) services enable you to bid on top-ranking spots for the selected keywords. You pay the amount you bid when a visitor searches for the keyword(s) you bid on and clicks through to your site.

Google AdWords and Yahoo! Search Marketing are the two most popular PPC programs. However, advertising on these two PPC search engines is expensive, and your AdSense earnings will likely not cover the advertising costs.

There are alternatives, such as Bidvertiser.com, Adbrite.com, Findology.com, etc. Bidvertiser.com and Adbrite.com are significantly less expensive than Google AdWords and

Yahoo Search Marketing, so I suggest you promote with them initially.

Adbrite.com and Bidvertiser.com are not search engines. When you sign up to advertise with them, they will distribute your contextual advertisements to the categories and websites of your choosing inside their network.

You will, without a doubt, promote on those linked categories and high-traffic websites. You should also consider selecting these unconnected categories, which may offer targeted traffic and improve your AdSense earnings.

Do not bid excessively high. Six to nine cents should be sufficient to get hundreds of targeted visitors to your website within a few days. You may continue your ad campaigns as long as your daily AdSense earnings exceed your advertising expenses.

RSS advertising

RSS advertising is an accessible approach to increasing your website's exposure. By producing an RSS file and uploading it to RSS directories and search engines, the links to your website's content will show in front of users who use RSS readers or news aggregators, thereby bringing targeted visitors to your website. Need further clarification? You can visit Google and enter "create an RSS feed" as a search keyword.

You will find comprehensive explanations of RSS and step-by-step instructions on constructing an RSS file to improve website traffic. It will take you many days to master and fully comprehend RSS. Using free software tools, some RSS sites provide a simple way to generate RSS files without an understanding of HTML coding.

Provide great content

Writing and submitting articles to free content platforms is another free technique to improve website traffic. If your content is impressive, your articles can attract thousands of visitors to your website in weeks.

There are additional effective strategies to improve website traffic. Search engines offer free information and resources on website marketing and promotion. The greater the number of visitors you can generate for your website, the greater your AdSense earnings will be.

CHAPTER 10

VIDEO TALK REVIEW

M any people have or are interested in finding a network marketing opportunity that allows them to earn money by selling products or services they appreciate. With so much competition, standing out from the crowd can be challenging. My Video Talk offers you the ideal option and chance. This section examines the company, what they offer and whether or not its program is profitable.

Mel and Amy Gill established Team Effort International in 2002 and are the My Video Talks studio creators. They are a global firm with a significant overseas following, and in 2004 it established a division in the United States just outside the San Francisco Bay Area. In April 2010, My Video Talk Studio began its pre-launch phase.

The company aims to develop cutting-edge communications technology to revolutionize global connections, communications, education, and marketing. Their live video streaming technology enables direct contact that is swift, streamlined, and effective.

The Service

The Studio is meant to help individuals, businesses, and marketers stand out from the competition, increase sales and strengthen customer connections by making video the focal point of their communications rather than text.

My Video Talk Studio consists of the following:

My Video Designer - Create and send branded video e-mails in minutes without the need for coding or technological expertise. Each email video can be completely personalized with images, logos, and banners.

My Video Broadcaster - Enables you to host live streaming video webinars and share PowerPoint presentations and other videos and files, all within a branded framework that can be fully customized.

My Video Channel - Enables you to create customizable web videos, branded for you and your company and free of rival or third-party advertisements.

My Video Webshow - Enables HD video conferencing with up to seven participants within an entirely branded and customizable framework.

Each product in the suite is fully customizable and incorporates SEO optimization by default. The company offers a Live Learning Channel via which members can receive one-on-one instruction or participate in webinars and conferences.

Compensation Scheme

My Video Talk's basic membership begins at $249.90 and requires a $29.00 monthly cost. A Business Builders membership is also available for $399.90 plus $49.00 monthly.

Six of the eight ways to generate money are bonuses you receive for increasing sales volumes and recruiting new members to help the business expand. You earn $25.00 for each sold Basic package and $100.00 per sold Business Builders package. Residual income is calculated using a mechanism known as Dual Core Double Binary Compensation.

While studying the company, I was pretty dissatisfied to find that the four enormous images that symbolize the components of My Talk Video on their homepage appeared to be interactive but did nothing when clicked. In addition, the examples on the product page were photos rather than films demonstrating the look and feel. However, their primary Product Video was well-made.

As internet usage continues to increase and more businesses, consumers, and entrepreneurs utilize modern communication technology, My Talk Video is well-positioned to profit from this trend. Individuals with the necessary marketing skills should be able to profit from their business so long as they can expand their staff proportionally.

Managing a network marketing firm is difficult enough without having to sell to uninterested family, friends, and acquaintances. Suppose you are serious about making a substantial income with this or any other MLM business. In that case, you need to learn how the pros advertise My Video Talk and how they generate massive downlines and profits fast and effectively.

CHAPTER 11

RESIDENTIAL CLEANING SERVICE

Unlike what you may believe, starting a house cleaning service is probably not quite as tricky as you think. If you have basic cleaning skills, you can offer a service to others that will generate a lucrative side income or possibly a full-time salary.

You may believe you must launch a small business and complete a lot of paperwork. This may be useful if you intend to work with companies, but it is not required. In reality, you can offer your house cleaning services to people who cannot or do not choose to clean their homes.

For tax purposes, you must receive cash compensation. This is not a difficult obstacle to overcome. Simply spread the news among your relatives and friends. They will inform their friends about your service, and word might spread rapidly.

The initial investment is small, yet the profit potential is substantial. The benefit of launching a cleaning service is that once you acquire a few regular clients, they will continue to use your services.

If you want to expand your house cleaning service to include small businesses, you will need to consider incorporating them. You must defend yourself against lawsuits and reduce your tax liability. Also, incorporating your house cleaning service is not as difficult as you might believe.

Simply conduct a little research on Google, and you will find some incorporation firms that would be pleased to help you establish your house cleaning service. This will enable you to accept any kind of payment, and the customer will be able to deduct it from their taxes.

Owning your house cleaning service may be pretty lucrative if you stick with it and do a good job, regardless of whether you incorporate or accept cash.

CHAPTER 12

VAN RENTAL SERVICE

While many businesses and services provide rental vehicles, many do not offer support. Establishing a "guy with a van" service is one method you can profitably utilize the van you own for jobs that require additional assistance. Customers may choose your services if they cannot handle some components of a move or item transportation on their own.

Renting a vehicle from a major company can often be prohibitively expensive. Even using a van for a few hours from a local firm may be costly. When you can offer a better bargain to persons needing this service, you can start a small business or earn extra money on the side. To further compete with the competition, you may offer your services after other companies have sent their employees home.

Who Needs Van Service?

Moving firms are renowned for packaging, loading, and transferring products from one location to another. For a local relocation, a "guy with a van" service may be what a family needs to stay within its budgetary constraints. Occasionally, using the van is all required; therefore, you may offer two distinct services: van-only service and van-with-help service.

As college students enter the sphere of higher education, some students remain close to home. It may be impossible for the family vehicle to transport all their possessions to the college campus. The temporary rental of a van is ideal for minimizing the number of visits to and from the university.

Spring cleaning might often necessitate transporting un-wanted items to the Salvation Army, Goodwill, a local charity, or a junkyard. Used couches, dining room tables, and other large home items cannot fit in a car's trunk, necessitating a larger vehicle's employment. A "guy with a van" service helps individuals load these products and deliver them to their location for a nominal price.

A van is also required when substantial household items are purchased from a furniture store, and there are no oth-er means to bring them home. A "guy with a van" service eliminates this issue and assists customers in getting their belongings safely inside their homes.

To pique the public's interest in your van services, you must make them aware that they exist. When folks require assistance or the services of another, the local Yellow Pages is one of the most often used resources. It is highly recom-mended that you place an advertisement or listing with this source to make your business more competitive.

Also, the local newspaper is traditional advertising that helps generate business. In addition, while you travel about town in your van, the public will become aware of your ser-vices due to the eye-catching advertising displayed on its side.

Once your reputation has been established, word of mouth will spread. If you provide a decent service, you can consider growing your firm and hiring other personnel to serve more locations; then, the world is your oyster!

CHAPTER 13

A SHOP SELLING USED BOOKS

Everyone disapproves of the idea of selling used books. However, the local yellow pages can be found in any major city worldwide. There are between three and five significant bookshops that specialize in the sale of used books. In certain places, there are retail malls, including exclusively secondhand bookstores arranged adjacently. It is also advantageous from a financial standpoint.

This business can be started either full or part-time. Selling secondhand or used books typically takes five years to become solidly established. Once these five years have passed, it will be possible to earn at least $50,000 every year.

Where are your stores located?

Look for a city or town with a population of at least 100,000 and at least two or three colleges or universities. Choose a store with affordable rent near these universities but situate it in a high-traffic location or close to other bookstores.

How to purchase old books

There are wholesalers of used books. A Google search can reveal some wholesale secondhand book suppliers. By requesting information, learn how to order used books from a bookstore that specializes in them.

Also, promote locally in the classifieds of your local newspaper that you would buy used books. Few flyers in your local libraries and college campuses offer you the opportunity to purchase and sell used books.

When people clear out their attics, they may wish to dispose of books stored there for decades. A classified advertisement in your local newspaper can deliver the books to your shop for pennies. Inexpensive flyers can be made at a local rapid print shop and distributed or placed beneath the windshields of vehicles in the parking lots of major shopping centers.

Generally, advertising and special offers around holidays such as Christmas, Mother's Day, and Father's Day are very efficient at attracting new clients to your store. Few used book businesses have gotten old manuscripts in this manner.

Create a welcoming atmosphere and open invitation for browsers, price your inventory reasonably, prioritize personalized service and let word-of-mouth advertising and time do the rest.

10% to 15% of the price of a new book should be applied to the cost of your old books.

Avoid reading explicit sexually-oriented publications.

The following kind of books are prevalent:

- Development, time management, and people management.

- You can find self-help and self-improvement manuals, mail orders, auto repair, carpentry, metals, house construction, gardening and company start-up, and culinary arts publications.

- World War II, history, aviation, sports, women's romance, science fiction, mysteries, and historical and ancient manuscripts.

What will it cost to open a second-hand bookstore? There may be approximately $50,000 in start-up expenses.

CHAPTER 14

MAKE YOUR OWN TEETH-WHITENING SYSTEM

As with many people, biannual cleanings may be the extent of your relationship with your dentist. Every day, people of all ages purchase goods to whiten their teeth and improve their smiles from local retailers. Once you have a passion for helping others, a restricted budget does not impede owning your own teeth whitening machine.

Location, business plan, and promotion are in place, and you are well on earning money by providing teeth whitening services. While others are spending hundreds of dollars, your consumers will realize they are saving a substantial amount of money by visiting you.

The initial investment will necessitate lightweight and individualized client kits. Other expenses will include comfortable chairs, safety eyewear, and cleaning supplies. You must ask your supplier how long the light will last and how much a replacement would cost.

Imagine your clientele paying for their regular salon treatments and running into individuals who have used your whitening technique. Not only will they be captivated, but they may also take a little more time to examine the typical outcomes.

Teeth whitening is prevalent today, and you will likely have more customers for this service than for your primary business! Like a gorgeous hairstyle, a sparkling grin will result in instant referrals. Visual sales are made when a person enjoys the appearance of another individual.

People have become weary of attempting to whiten their teeth at home. The procedure can take days or weeks, and it is often difficult to detect changes. A whitening technique delivers instantaneous results that they will find satisfactory. This will benefit your bottom line, as satisfied consumers will refer more business to you. When your firm grows, your profit will inevitably increase as well.

You may not believe you can afford your whitening system as a small business. Perhaps you are searching for company startup options. Your search is at an end. With start-up expenditures of as little as one or two thousand dollars, virtually anyone can undertake this endeavor.

You will begin making a profit quickly and can purchase additional products with the money you earn without having to invest hundreds of dollars. You will also be able to expand your business.

Among the main reasons to have your system are the following:

- You can use it yourself
- You can offer promotional gifts
- After a minimal setup fee, profit is anticipated in as little as one month.
- Gain more customers by offering different services.

People strive to keep the perfect appearance regardless of their means. Your financial future would suffer if you did not possess your teeth-whitening system. What are you expecting? If you are weary of working for someone else or simply want to earn more money in your present business, you have found the answer!

CHAPTER 15

A FREE WEBSITE BUILDER APPLICATION

Your website is like a storefront where all your products and services are displayed for all viewing and purchasing. Your website consists of web pages stored on a web host to deliver sales messages and collect leads.

Most of your actions, including list building, opt-in forms, traffic generation, and persuasive sales letters, direct your prospects to your website.

Some people find designing web pages a nightmare, while others find it enjoyable. Some webmasters have specialized in software such as Microsoft FrontPage, Dreamweaver, etc., but never used the Free Website Builder Software.

Technicality:

This free web builder program is meant to save you the trouble of learning HTML - absolutely no HTML knowledge is necessary; what you see is what you get. It is simple and comes with a free video tutorial and step-by-step guide.

Cost/Time Aspects:

When it comes to DIY to save time and money, you cannot afford to be without this free site builder software that includes over 100+ free professional website templates. The free website builder has built-in FTP software for instant publishing with a single click. It is an entirely professional version with no required upgrade.

Security:

The security of the free software is uncompromised, and you do not anticipate receiving any spam because it is Strong security-certified and 100% Clean with Absolutely No Spyware, Adware, or virus.

Flexibility:

The web pages are Search Engine Friendly; they are easily crawlable by Search Engines such as Google, MSN, Yahoo, etc., which are the primary source of traffic for most websites on the Internet. By designing a search engine-friendly website, you will rank higher in search engines and attract more visitors who can be converted into clients.

Monetization:

Free Website Builder is branded to generate revenue when shared with others. It offers an Integrated Free Money-Making Opportunity in which you can make money like crazy for free. In my days on the Internet, I often cracked jokes about anything free, but today I have significantly benefited from free and valuable software such as this.

CHAPTER 16

MAILINGS

For years, whenever we pick up a tabloid or newspaper, there is a good possibility that we will see an advertisement claiming that we can earn thousands of dollars stuffing envelopes from the comfort of our own homes.

We know these claims are overstated, and you will never earn that much money as a third-party mailer. Despite this, the premise is sound, although the execution is not. Accurate direct mailing is a service you can give directly to businesses with minimal equipment and little knowledge.

Businesses constantly outsource labor. You probably already know someone who outsources for a company. Daily, accountants, attorneys, and even housekeeping personnel provide services to organizations via outsourcing. Direct mail operates similarly. Most firms distribute periodicals to their customers, clients, and workers.

These are typical, one-size-fits-all mailings that can be expensive and time-consuming to send in-house. By outsourcing, businesses can pay you to manage their mailings, maintain a database of their mailing lists and ensure that these tasks are completed within their specified time limit.

You only need a computer, a decent printer for address labels, and plenty of free time. Direct mailing enables you to transform the old scam of envelope stuffing into a legitimate and lucrative enterprise. Today, you may be your boss with direct mail.

Try what I did if you need money immediately or within the hour. I am making more money today than I did in my previous business, and you can, too, if you click the link below and read the incredible accurate tale. I was suspicious for only ten seconds after joining before I knew what this was. You will also be beaming from ear to ear, as I was.

CHAPTER 17

BLOGGING

With the proper tools, blogging can be a simple online endeavor. Sign up for a blogging platform as your first step. Blogger.com is one of the largest sites, receives a TON of traffic, and is entirely free. After registering, you should immediately make your first post and ensure it is on-topic.

Next, you should sign up for a free AdSense account. Here is where you can earn money with your internet hustle. You may not become wealthy with sufficient traffic, but you can make a little additional cash on the side. AdSense essentially places advertisements on your blog.

"Affiliate Marketing" is another online blogging enterprise you could pursue. You can create a blog on any particular topic that interests you. You could, for instance, be interested in golf or any other sport. Then, you may enroll in an affiliate scheme that sells golf and sporting goods. After creating your golf-related blog article, you might include your affiliate link. Even slightly, people will not bother reading your site if you appear dishonest.

Creating a blog is the most superficial aspect of this internet endeavor. Next, you must determine how to attract traffic. I recall reading an article stating that over 70,000 blogs are established daily. Thus, you must compete with this traffic to make your site stand out.

Most blog platforms allow you to customize the layout, so ensure it looks excellent. Avoid blue lettering on a red backdrop, as this appears unprofessional and tacky; instead, make the text easy on the eyes.

Remember the most crucial guideline of internet communication: "Keep Everything Relevant and on Topic." You cannot have a blog about keeping frogs as pets and attempt to advertise a boot-selling affiliate network. You can have countless blogs on various themes circulating the Internet. Monetizing your blog makes it capable of earning cash for you. There are many methods for monetizing blogs, but contextual advertising solutions are the most prevalent.

A contextual advertising system examines the content of your blog. It uses keywords to return advertisements to the blog page based on what the user is viewing, thereby delivering ads that are more relevant to your blog content and, as a result, are likely to be clicked by users.

Each click on one of these advertisements produces revenue for you. Upon registering or opening a free account with any contextual ads service provider, you will be issued a unique code that you just copy and paste onto your blog. At that point, the system will begin delivering these highly targeted advertisements.

Google AdSense, Yahoo! Publisher Network, Microsoft adCenter, AOL sponsored listings, Kontera, etc., are contextual advertising service providers.

Installing affiliate links on blogs is another prevalent method of blog monetization. Affiliate links are typically image-only, text-only, or image-plus-text advertisements placed on a blog by the blogger on behalf of online retailers or marketers.

These links, when clicked, lead the user to the merchant's or advertiser's website; if a sale, action, or lead is made, this can be traced back to the referral site, which is the blog from which the user entered the merchant's website; the blogger receives a commission for this sale, action or lead.

As a blogger, you must register for free with any affiliate network to access a vast array of fantastic products and services to promote and earn commissions per sale, action, or lead.

After registration, you will get a unique ID, which will be incorporated into the affiliate links for any items or services you want to promote on your site. This unique ID makes it easy to attribute any sale, action, or lead to you as the referrer.

After registering, you can browse the network for fantastic items or services to promote, especially ones relevant to your blog's topic. You'll be presented with codes, including your unique ID, that you copy and paste on your site.

The affiliate link will subsequently be displayed on the blog. ClickBank, commission junction, ShareASale, AzoogleAds, hydra network, never blue, etc., are affiliate networks that provide access to many excellent products and services for promotion.

Due to the enormous number of products and services accessible on various affiliate networks can be challenging to search for. To simplify the process, you can use a service such as an offer vault, which finds the top-paying offers and arranges them by niche.

You can also monetize your blog by renting out advertising space directly to retailers and advertisers. However, this monetization is only effective if your blog is highly famous and receives a lot of traffic. No advertiser will be ready to pay for exposure on a site where few people see their ads. When you establish this revenue source, though, you will begin to earn more than you do from contextual and affiliate advertisements.

Monthly, interested merchants or advertisers pay you directly to place their advertisements on your blog. Create "advertise here" spots on your blog so that advertisers can see what you are offering. Ensure that your advertising rates are competitive, taking your blog's statistics (or traffic) and what your competitors are offering into mind.

Simply put, the greater your blog's statistics, the more desirable your ad space becomes. Displaying your blog's statistics on your "advertise here" page or areas could attract advertisers and help you justify your advertising charges.

You must also integrate online payment processors, such as PayPal, alert pay, liberty reserve, etc., into your blog so that you may receive payment from interested advertisers without difficulty. You can also accept credit card payments, but your blog must have a secure platform for credit card transactions for you to do so.

Directly selling your items or services or those for which you have reselling rights is the fourth way to monetize your blog. These goods and services may include software, eBooks, audio and video CDs, Webhosting, and graphic design.

You can sell virtually anything if your products are relevant to your blog's content. Again, as with renting ad space, you must provide your blog with a simple method of accepting online payment from potential purchasers.

CHAPTER 18

MAKING MONEY THROUGH ART

M aking money with art is not as simple as it may appear. The strategies and methods that led to success are as involved as the creation of the art itself. This section offers seven suggestions for earning money through art.

Network

Networking is vital for freelance graphic designers because it can lead to business prospects through friends, family, former clients, etc.

Joining design communities in your area and attending local events can open doors to new opportunities and be quite beneficial. You may demonstrate your presence in the design community by doing so. In today's society, social media also plays a significant part in professional networking.

Twitter, LinkedIn, and Facebook are some well-known social networking platforms. Through various media sites, designers can develop a solid network of clients, coworkers, friends, and other designers.

Maintain relationships.

Attempting to maintain ties with clients once a project has been completed is equally as vital as acquiring new ones. By establishing secure, long-term connections with clients, you may earn their loyalty for future ventures and receive referrals from them.

Differentiation

Customers are often willing to offer a premium for items that stand out. Making yourself and your design work stand out might provide similar outcomes. Try to distinguish your approach and style from that of your competition so that you can charge more.

Multitasking

Clients may view you as a more valuable asset if you diversify your skill set and display proficiency in different areas of graphic design. Although it is crucial to specialize in a single area of graphic design, the ability to assist in other areas makes you a more desirable job applicant. You must be familiar with the basics of many sectors related to your employment, such as website design, copywriting, and printing.

Try maintaining your logo, brochure, and website design abilities and knowledge. This should increase your marketability and give you access to additional clients and projects.

Offer Extra Services

You may want to offer bonus services in addition to your standard design services; this sets you apart from your competitors and allows you to decide the right price for such a service, resulting in a profit.

People and decision-makers are always looking for free items. Therefore, these add-on services could be a deal-breaker. This could be accomplished, for instance, by offering many benefits for the price of one, such as: acquiring a website design and receiving a free logo.

Differentiate Your Clientele

You should maintain special pay rates for small, medium, and large companies. Smaller businesses cannot afford the same rates as larger businesses. Hence they require different rates. Since you want your services to be accessible to companies of all sizes, you should devise criteria for establishing variable pricing based on business categorization. Keeping your services accessible to a diverse clientele will help you earn money through art.

Sharing information

Share your experience and knowledge with others. This allows you to learn more and concentrate on enhancing your abilities. For instance, you can offer your expertise by publishing articles in your field of expertise. Many graphic designers do so by use of blogs. You can earn money while gaining experience to add to your graphic design portfolio.

CHAPTER 19

FREELANCING

Freelance employment is becoming much more popular than traditional jobs. People motivated by the desire to be self-employed often find online freelancing a convenient means of becoming self-employed.

Computer programming, graphic arts, computer programming, photography and picture retouching, web design, copywriting, and editing are in high demand in the freelancing market. Writing and editing are the best-paying freelance professions. After writing, web design and graphics are the most lucrative freelancing professions.

If self-employment is the goal, freelancing is one of the quickest and least expensive methods to get started. Print, word-of-mouth, past employers, and classified advertisements can be used to locate freelance jobs; online agencies and marketplace-style job websites are the most recent Internet contributions to this expanding area.

Freelancing job search websites such as Freelancer.com, Guru.com, eLance.com, and oDesk.com have proliferated, offering organizations access to a competitive pool of contractors who submit bids and applications in response to job ads on the site. This allows the contracting organization to select freelancers based on their skills, applications, and recommendations instead of their geographic location.

Some jobs have a predetermined fee, while others are billed hourly as the project continues. Due to the internet nature of most freelancing employment, skilled professionals and enthusiastic amateurs can be recruited from anywhere in the world.

Freelancers with more significant experience and competence in their chosen field often charge more for their services and make their portfolios accessible to prospective clients via their websites or agency profiles.

Most professionals begin their freelancing careers by working for an agency or another company, developing their credibility, portfolio, and relationships as they accomplish assignments within their chosen sector. Since much freelance work is completed on the contractor's own time, it is easy to continue working at one's primary job while growing a clientele and accumulating expertise.

Businesses that utilize freelancers enjoy many benefits. The only way to acquire the specialized abilities required for a particular project is for the period of employment, with no further obligation. One element that motivates organizations to consider contracting out work is the cost savings realized by not providing benefits to freelance workers. Online freelance employees have proven to be the primary profit generators for many businesses.

There are advantages to working as a freelancer online: no travel expenses are required, travel time is saved, and you are the boss and in charge. You can earn more money by working longer hours or serving more customers.

However, there are disadvantages to relying solely on freelance work for a living. The freelancer is responsible for locating, applying to, and negotiating job terms, and there is no assurance of a sufficient amount of available work.

The convenience of working from home can lead to complacency, and a decline in output and clients have the right to suspend work at any moment. Efforts should be made to have as little downtime between jobs as feasible. A sufficient number of contracts going steadily through the application and production processes will help.

The reality is that there are a large number of online free-lancers but just a small number of successful online freelancers. To be a successful online freelancer, you must possess a skill or set of skills in demand.

Independent contractors must find a means to attract clients. This is the greatest obstacle for those who are new to freelancing. Also, freelancers must possess strong communication skills, be self-motivated, and be committed to offering quality services.

Before starting work as a freelancer, it is necessary to understand the hurdles that freelancing or starting your own business can present. Knowing how some freelancers achieved online success is beneficial. Also, you should be aware of the common causes of failure in online freelancing. You can speak with freelancers who have been in the field for years and read articles, forum postings, and success stories.

If you begin freelancing online without developing skills and understanding the facts of freelancing online, your attempt may be another failure. Conduct research, be willing to work hard, and be persistent and diligent. Those characteristics that make a great employee also make a successful freelancer.

Top ten freelancer marketplaces online.

Since seven years ago, I have been a skilled internet marketer in many online freelance marketplaces. When I first began freelancing online, I relied on a single platform for all my work. I made enough money to pursue my career without difficulty.

When I began working for other websites, I got substantially higher-paying freelance employment. Let me provide my perspective on the ten best freelancing marketplaces among the hundreds of online freelancing marketplaces.

1) Upwork.com

This website combines the two most popular freelance marketplaces, oDesk, and Elance. Here, a freelancer can find virtually all internet work opportunities. There are two types of employment. One is an hourly position, while the other is a fixed-price position.

2) Freelancer.com

Another central online freelance marketplace is Freelancer. com. A freelancer can find employment from data input to advanced programming. There are thousands of clients and independent contractors across the globe. Here, new freelancer can simply find their desired jobs.

3) Fiverr.com

Fiverr.com is, in my opinion, one of the most prominent online freelancing markets. Here, a freelancer must publish a gig with detailed guidelines regarding what services they can give. If the client approves, they can begin ordering for five bucks so that the client can quickly get quality services at a low cost. For this reason, this website's popularity is increasing daily.

4) PeoplePerHour.com

PeoplePerHour.com is an excellent platform for freelance online work. If you are a digital marketer, article writer, graphic designer, web developer, or SEO professional, or if you enjoy working with anything else, your specialty is digital marketing, article writing, graphic design, or web development. PeoplePerHour is certainly worth investigating. You must publish hourly, and clients will pay you according to your established fee.

5) 99designs.com

This is a forum for freelance designers; 99designs.com allows you to compete in design contests and receive feedback as clients select the winning designs and pay well. It's an excellent method for skilled designers to demonstrate their abilities and make a handsome income.

6) iWriter.com

iWritter.com is the premier online marketplace for freelance content writers. This is the most efficient, convenient, and dependable method for getting website content. A freelancer can also make approximately $15 per decent piece.

7) Independent Writing Jobs.com

This is another well-known marketplace for freelance writers, bloggers, editors, and publishers. This is an excellent alternative for freelancers with a knack for language.

8) Toptal.com

Toptal.com is one of the most prominent freelance markets for custom software development projects. A client who desires a custom software development service can have one from a highly qualified and seasoned independent contractor.

9) Project for hire.com

With many project categories, Project4hire.com makes it simple to find projects that match your skill set without requiring you to sift through massive amounts of job postings. It benefits authors, coders, consultants, designers, and programmers.

10) iFreelance.com

The iFreelance.com platform is home to some of the regular suspects in the world of freelancing. Here you will find proofreading, artwork, data entry, graphic design, photography, and any other form of professional assignment. The site is not, however, free for freelancers. There will be an associated membership charge.

Therefore, you can select one of these online freelance marketplaces to begin your freelancing career or to complete a project quickly. Here, you will discover freelancers and clients from all over the world. What are you waiting for? Start your career off right with these.

CHAPTER 20

ONLINE TUTORING

If you have teaching expertise and enjoy assisting others in their education, you can make money teaching online. Many companies will pay you to help children and adults study from the comfort of your own home. Depending on the industry you work with and the subjects you teach, you can earn anywhere from $10 and $40 per hour.

Most online teaching jobs demand a bachelor's degree or current university enrolment. A few businesses, including eSylvan, require a valid teaching certificate. Visit the websites of each company to view their qualifications. Consider volunteering in a library, school, or organization that needs tutors if you have the knowledge but lack the expertise.

The companies offer both part-time and full-time employment. Typically, the number of hours you work is variable, but you must be accessible in the afternoons and evenings after school has ended. Your employer will match your abilities with children who require assistance in those areas. After being paired with a student, you collaborate with them utilizing an online whiteboard and chat window.

You and the learner can write or draw simultaneously on the same screen. You can communicate using the chat window.

Specific online teaching organizations allow you to assist any student who requests assistance with their assignments. You have the opportunity to work with different pupils and will likely be kept busy throughout the week. You need not be concerned about cancellations.

Other organizations will pair you directly with students whom you will regularly tutor. Working with the same students can be enjoyable since you can track their progress and tailor your coaching to their preferred learning styles.

Consider working for yourself if you value flexibility. It may take time to attract high-quality clients, but you can set your fees without dealing with an intermediary. Make relationships by volunteering in your community, requesting client referrals, and placing advertising in your local newspaper or on Craigslist. This allows you the option of combining in-person tuition with online instruction.

Teaching online is an excellent method to generate money for stay-at-home parents, people searching for a second job, and people who love teaching but are not employed in the school system.

You can begin this project in different ways, such as by creating a YouTube channel, a podcast, or a blog. However, I'd want to introduce you to three additional strategies to leverage your unfair advantage (teaching what you already know). This is the most acceptable option to earn extra money or a living.

Check out these three online teaching platforms:

Udemy.com - Based in San Francisco, California, Udemy provides over 20,000 courses in every possible subject area. The exciting part is that you can pick your fee, choose your topic and keep 100 percent of the profit if you help market your course. If Udemy sells your course and gets you, students, you will receive fifty percent of the income. The average instructor on Udemy earns $7,000. Ninety-six percent of teachers generate revenue.

Skillshare.com is a community for online learning. You can also become a teacher on the platform and make supplemental income depending on what you already know, enjoy, or are passionate about.

Do you have a design, gaming, or programming experience? Then instruct it. They have more than 750,000 students and have compensated their teachers with over $3 million. The average salary of a teacher exceeds $3,500. Then why are you still waiting?

Dabble.co - If you prefer a more hands-on approach to instruction, then this platform is for you. Depending on where you live, you register to teach classes in your local community.

You can teach anywhere, including coffee shops and restaurants. Anyone is permitted to lead classes (which means you). You can participate in a class, teach a lesson or host a course in which someone else teaches.

CHAPTER 21

TESTING WEBSITES ONLINE

In a world of phony online job opportunities, it's reassuring to know there are a few legitimate online side hustles you can pursue to make a decent side income. Website testing is one particular example. If you've never attempted it before, now is an excellent opportunity to learn what it is, how much you may potentially earn, and who will pay you to get started.

Website testing is invaluable in today's market, as websites play a vital role in the ability of both small and large organizations to reach, engage and convert online customers. It is not sufficient to have a website; the site must be developed to create fantastic brand associations and drive profitable conversions.

Considering how much money and time brands invest in web design and development, it becomes clear why they emphasize testing. Even though every circumstance is unique, below are a few average costs associated with designing a bespoke website:

- Small enterprise website: $2,000 to $8,000
- Medium-sized enterprise website: $10,000 to $25,000
- $5,000 to $40,000 for an e-commerce website.
- Large enterprise website: $25,000 to $40,000

Thus, these are merely the costs associated with launching a business. When other fees such as domain name, SSL certificate, web hosting, content management system, constant web design, advertising, and optimization are factored in, the monthly expenses might reach thousands of dollars.

If a business invests in a website, it must be functional. There are many methods for determining the functionality of a website, but nothing surpasses the raw, unfiltered nature of user testing.

How Much Can You Help Make Website Testing?

Let's be clear: You will not become wealthy in testing websites, at least in this capacity. For most people, website testing is not intended as a full-time occupation and will not significantly affect their income.

It can, however, supplement your cash flow and give you a small amount of additional spending money for the weekend, the week after a holiday, or a significant purchase without draining your savings.

Most website testing companies will generally pay you $10 per test website. Occasionally, you may receive $15 to $25, but these are rare instances and are often reserved for individuals with expertise. A typical website testing session lasts between 15 and 30 minutes, while a few can be completed in as little as 10 minutes.

In many instances, website testing opportunities are communicated to end users by email or online, and you must "claim" the test to gain access. Depending on the number of users competing for opportunities, it may be more challenging to receive testing with some companies than with others.

If you receive five offers to test websites daily, you will likely only claim one or two and need to act quickly. However, an extra $10 each day can quickly accumulate. If you evaluate five websites each week at that rate, you may expect to earn an additional $200 per month.

CHAPTER 22

BUYING DIRT-CHEAP AUTOMOBILES AND REPAIRING THEM

In today's market, finding alternative ways to earn income outside your primary occupation is sometimes vital. For many people, this side business is purchasing cars at rock-bottom prices, repairing them, and reselling them to people who need vehicles for a considerable profit.

If you are mechanically savvy or eager to learn and need additional cash to pay bills, save for a kid, or relocate, flipping dirt-cheap automobiles may be the side hustle you need to get started. It would help if you only located these automobiles. Continue reading to discover where you may get inexpensive dirt cars to patch up.

The Local Publication

The local newspaper is one of the finest places to get inexpensive dirt automobiles. Often, individuals sell cars at As Is pricing with no warranty of operability. Suppose you can purchase these automobiles for just a few hundred dollars and find a means to acquire inexpensive parts to replace and still generate a profit. In that case, you stand a good chance of doubling your initial investment.

The Wheeler Dealer and Comparable Works

There is a great chance your community has a free local magazine devoted solely to vehicles and the steps required to sell, purchase or exchange a car. These magazines allow individuals to list wanted ads, sales ads, and other adverts, and companies to demonstrate their support for the community and boost their exposure by purchasing ad space.

This is an excellent way to get dirt cheap cars with an "As Is" price tag and an even better way to acquire dirt cheap cars than the traditional ads. This area is reserved only for car-related businesses, allowing individuals to connect easily with others in the same industry. It is crucial to locate these papers in your town and understand how to use them to your advantage if you are interested in starting a small business.

Monthly auctions are held at police impound lots, where one can find affordable automobiles. You can check eBay, Craigslist, and new car lots.

New automobile dealerships accept trade-ins that they know will be difficult to sell. Insurance companies are another excellent source for inexpensive automobiles, as they will generally purchase a vehicle from a client when it costs more to repair than to scrap.

CHAPTER 23

FOREX TRADING

Forex trading online has many benefits, especially for beginners. Many people in this country have invested in it either as a side hustle or full-time employment over the previous decade. If you take the time to grasp its nitty-gritty details, you have a strong possibility of generating gains that could even exceed your income from your day job.

Even though becoming a professional online Forex trader can take a considerable time, the fundamental fundamentals are simple to grasp. Accessing the Forex market and initiating trading is similarly quick and straightforward.

It can be done from anywhere with a computer and an internet connection. You can engage in transactions with minimal expense and effort through relevant financial institutions or brokers.

A further advantage of online Forex trading is the market's excellent liquidity. This market allows currency purchases and sales anytime, regardless of market conditions. This is in contrast to equities, with which you are virtually stuck during volatile periods. Since there will always be a buyer in the Forex market, you are free to liquidate your position anytime.

Since it operates 24 hours a day, you will find Forex trading online to be a very lucrative endeavor. This market never sleeps, so it will be convenient for you if you have other responsibilities and can only trade part-time. This is because you can choose the most suitable trade time to avoid interfering with your daily schedule.

To start trading as a beginner on the Forex market, you will not require a significant initial investment. Unlike other assets such as stocks, futures, and options, starting as a currency trader will not require a substantial investment. Certain brokers offer micro-trading accounts with a $100 minimum deposit requirement.

As a novice trader, it is recommended that you open an online Forex trading account with a minimal minimum. This makes this investment more accessible to individuals who lack substantial initial cash.

The opportunity to trade with leverage is an additional benefit of online Forex trading. You can utilize a small deposit to manage a much bigger total contract value. Using leverage, you can earn substantial earnings while keeping your risk capital to a minimum.

For example, if you trade with a leverage of 1:100, a 100 USD deposit would let you purchase or sell 10,000 USD worth of currencies. However, you must employ leverage with extreme caution since an improper application can result in enormous losses.

CHAPTER 24

STOCK PHOTOGRAPHIC IMAGES

Many individuals work primarily to earn money, but this may not provide them with happiness. However, some are fortunate enough to gain money by pursuing their love. One of these methods is photography. Some photographers have received professional training.

Typically, they are affiliated with an agency or work independently, but there are many more, like you and I, who like photographing people, objects, and events. Here is your opportunity to make money from your pastime. The universe of stock photos is yours to explore.

Before we discuss how to generate money with this hobby, let's examine what stock photography is. It is the availability of licensed pictures for specific uses. You might be surprised by the demand for stock pictures. Graphic and website designers, online advertising agencies, and publishing companies demand them.

The best thing about stock photography is that you don't need to be a skilled photographer to make money with it. All that is required is a passion for photography mixed with imagination. Gradually, you will develop the ability to advertise yourself successfully and, as a result, earn money!

Some individuals may argue that stock photography pays little for individual images. However, those who complain about this see it as a situation where "the glass is half full." Authentic stock photographs may be purchased for as little as $1.

However, the reality is that many individuals can utilize a particular photograph. Combine this with the fact that the same image can be uploaded to many websites. A quick calculation reveals that this is a surefire way to earn a handsome sum! Today, some individuals can make a living from stock photography due to its enormous earning potential.

Now, how exactly can one make money with stock photography?

Here are a few suggestions for getting started. Creating an original collection of images is the most obvious initial step. Try to integrate a sense of originality into your captured images and perspectives.

You should consider the breadth of your intended collection. Some individuals prefer to specialize in a specific topic and become niche providers. Others want to cover a broad range of issues. Your decision is entirely up to you.

The next step in making money with stock photography is to create an online account with stock photography websites. Microstock photography firms are companies that accept images from different photographers, including amateurs and hobbyists.

They have a low-price, high-volume business model. ShutterStock.com, BigStockPhoto.com, Fotolia.com, 123rf.com, and Dreamstime.com are among the most renowned microstock websites.

With some of them, you can create an account. After this, an example folder is created. This is your opportunity to demonstrate your talent and be chosen. Select some of your finest images and upload them. Here is a helpful hint. Ensure that the titles of the photos you post are concise and pertinent. This can aid folks searching for images in swiftly locating relevant ones.

If you want to make money with stock photography, you should review the guidelines for each microstock site. These rules govern the images that may be posted and their dimensions, technical quality, and commercial feasibility.

Aim to upload a large number of high-quality images. This will improve the likelihood that your photos will be chosen and help you achieve your goal of earning money. Continue to add additional photos as time passes. You will realize that your hobby is a fantastic source of income.

CHAPTER 25

AFFILIATE MARKETING

Affiliate marketing is one of the most straightforward ways to generate revenue online. Consequently, why are so many affiliate marketers frustrated?

Recent holiday research indicates that online shopping has climbed by 12 percent and is projected to expand throughout 2009. Why are so many affiliates asking, If the earning potential has increased, how can one make money with affiliate marketing? Is it even still possible?

Affiliate marketing sales are on the rise. Therefore, it is achievable. Those who are successful, however, approach affiliate marketing quite differently than those who appear to be suffering. Here are five ways to generate money with affiliate marketing.

1. Pay close attention to trends. How people spend their money fluctuates with time; products and services that were in high demand one year may no longer fulfill consumers' needs.

You should keep your eyes and ears tuned to consumer and economic trends to comprehend how and where people spend their money. A visit to a bookstore and perusal of blogs and message boards will reveal what people invest their time and money in. This is advantageous while selecting affiliate programs.

2. Consider consumer feedback seriously. Marketers and advertising have less influence than they did a few decades ago. A basic advertisement is no longer as effec-

tive in affiliate marketing as it once was, but a consumer review can be.

Before enrolling in an affiliate program, you should read current consumer reviews. As part of your marketing strategy, make sure to solicit feedback from your list once you've signed up. Social networking and online forums are excellent locations to search for and request consumer evaluations.

3. Build your list. As the market evolves, making money through affiliate marketing without a list will become exceedingly tricky—however, not just any list but a responsive one. You desire a group of individuals who take your words seriously.

This indicates that you must focus on establishing trust. As an affiliate marketer, you merely direct individuals to valuable resources. However, to complete the sale, people must have faith in your recommendation.

4. Conduct more surveys. Those who profit from affiliate marketing understand their target market. They can better meet their needs because they are aware of them.

The most effective method for affiliate marketers to determine what their previous and future clients desire is to conduct surveys and polls. Whether the survey is a product review or an evaluation of your performance, the results provide insightful information on how to run your business more efficiently.

5. Team up. It is getting increasingly difficult for an individual to earn money through affiliate marketing on their own. More effort is required to surpass the competition, and more drive is needed to complete this work.

Working alongside another person or a group makes fulfilling an ever-growing list of tasks more manageable. You may choose to outsource duties, work with individuals in your sector or hire a business coach, but you must discover ways to utilize the abilities of others.

Affiliate marketing can be significantly less frustrating if you understand trends and your target market, establish a responsive list and leverage the abilities of others.

CHAPTER 26

PROMOTING GOOGLE ADSENSE ON YOUR SITE

For some time, many internet marketers have learned to earn additional income by enabling Google's AdSense Program to display targeted advertising on their websites, pushing various products for advertisers.

This has created a revenue stream that has considerably improved the advertiser's marketing efforts while also benefiting the webmaster who hosts these commercials, who receives a percentage of the cash whenever a website visitor clicks on the ads.

This is a win-win situation for all parties concerned, as the advertiser receives a potential sale, Google receives compensation, and the website advertising owner receives online revenue.

Google AdSense is a free tool that allows you to register an account and display relevant advertisements on your blog, website, or in free article directories. The advertisements are targeted, meaning that the information in the Google box is relevant to the products you are advertising on your website or the content you share.

This has also extended to the display of mobile and video advertisements; for instance, a website designed to sell golfing products will display AdSense advertisements on golfing techniques and other golf-related information. The publisher pays Google for the displayed advertisements targeted to their niche market.

The cash you earn through the AdSense program is the publisher's way of saying thank you for displaying their advertisement and driving traffic to it. Google is aware that visitors are typically attracted to high-quality content rather than a search listing and takes note of how descriptive the ad copy is on AdSense-enabled websites and blogs, for example:

Acting Positions Each month, 10,000 new job listings are posted. Today, find a job on Gumtree. Visit gumtree.com

Note how the website leverages material to market the idea of its benefits. This is a sales copy used by copywriters and publishers utilizing the AdSense program to generate cash online by understanding their target customers and creating highly effective advertisements.

Suppose your website generates a significant volume of focused traffic that converts effectively. In that case, AdSense may be an excellent idea and a terrific source of additional revenue. Still, if your website is failing to attract visitors, it is unlikely that AdSense would help.

Getting search engine optimization assistance and selecting the right keyword for your website content can make it easier for Google and the other search engines to locate you, increasing targeted traffic to your website.

Remember that AdSense and AdWords are distinct programs. People may purchase straight from the publisher using the selected term and enticing sales language, which is the beauty of AdWords.

AdSense employing baited sales copy, on the other hand, enables you to get online cash from individuals clicking on the advertisements. This is advantageous because AdSense connects you with those who are seeking information. AdSense will not only offer you more income, but it will also boost your website's visibility and search engine rankings.

CHAPTER 27

E-BOOK PUBLISHING

Today, there are many ways to make a living using the Internet. Some individuals sell stuff on auction platforms to earn a living, while others participate in freelance web content creation. Publishing eBooks online is one of the quickest ways for folks interested in generating digital material to earn money online. This online publication is the most excellent and fastest way to make money online.

Unlike written text in physical forms, such as books and magazines, ebooks can be published rapidly. As soon as the author completes authoring the e-book, they can take the necessary steps to get it published online.

Individuals can publish their ideas online as soon as they are ready, whether in the form of eBook publishing or otherwise. This rapid method of distributing this type of written material makes making and selling ebooks a quick way to earn money online.

Distributed to a Large Number of Individuals Immediately eBook publishing is the quickest way to make money online because this form of digital content can be given simultaneously to many consumers. Once the eBook has been entirely written, the following stage of publication is straightforward. Some persons will offer the product on their website, while others will utilize internet publishers to do the task.

Regardless of the chosen path, the eBook author will be able to offer all Internet users the chance to access and purchase their eBooks online. The more people who view and ultimately buy a published eBook online, the faster one will earn money.

Little to No Operating Costs Involved

Those considering eBook publishing as a way to earn a quick income online will also find that they can keep a large portion of the money provided to them by buyers, as there is little to no overhead.

All that is required for eBook creation and publishing is time, imagination, and possibly a modest price if employing an online publisher to promote the eBook. Therefore, the fewer expenses incurred, the more profit the eBook author will be able to retain.

Electronic books can be sold online continuously.

eBook publication is also a quick way to generate money online because, once created, the eBook can be sold online indefinitely, so long as the content does not become obsolete. This implies that the author of the eBook may sit back and relax, as the eBook will essentially sell itself.

In contrast to a web content writer who must regularly submit fresh pieces and is only compensated per article, eBook authors simply need to create the book once and have it sold repeatedly online, typically for a favorable price.

This is another significant reason why eBook publishing is the quickest way to make money online and something that all web content creators should consider doing.

CHAPTER 28

SELLING FORECLOSED PROPERTIES

B efore selling a foreclosed home, the first fundamental step a seller will do is to rid the property of clutter and dirt. The primary clients for this service are banks with a vast inventory of repossessed properties. The government also has many foreclosed properties for sale, making them customers.

If you have experience cleaning foreclosed homes, you know what to expect. Often, these properties are in such a horrible shape that the process can be highly challenging. Some homeowners vent their fury over foreclosure by inflicting damage on their foreclosed homes' walls, floors, and windows. Some individuals even leave the water running in the basement.

Guidelines for Establishing a Foreclosure Cleaning Service

You should begin there if you have not yet established licenses and insurance. You can get assistance from companies who are currently working on contracts. These professionals can steer you in the proper direction. A partnership with a junk hauling firm may follow. You will have much clearing if you get a contract to clean multiple foreclosed homes at once.

You need to know the pricing of this service to determine your price points. Pricing is typically determined by your location, the property's square footage, and the amount of time it has spent on the market. The longer a home has been vacant, the greater the likelihood of deterioration.

Consider forming strategic alliances with contractors and subcontractors. If you are cleaning foreclosed properties, you may as well offer handyman services. You may provide specialist services like pool cleaning.

Employ contractors or subcontractors to perform some cleaning and repair work. The amount you will charge property managers will be determined by the cost of recruiting personnel and the timeframe in which you can execute the job. Continually assess the property before providing an estimate.

CHAPTER 29

SELF-STORAGE AUCTIONS

Nationwide, every year (and especially during economic downturns), average individuals fail to make their monthly payments to Self-Storage facilities. Divorce, death, and job loss are just a few possible explanations.

However, when individuals fail to make these payments, the clock begins to tick. They are contacted and handed official documents and advertisements informing the globe that an absolute auction will be held to liquidate (sell) their possessions.

There are auction services that conduct 50 or more auctions daily, the vast majority of which are cash-only. All sales are final. You visit the apartment, it is opened, and the auctioneer begins the bidding. You have less than one minute to "review" the merchandise.

Typically, goods are stacked and packaged, and "difficult" to determine their genuine value (s). Bidding may last up to two minutes, after which you will hear SOLD! and move on to the next unit.

Bring your cash to the office, and within minutes you will be given 24-48 hours to remove your valuables. You must pay sales tax in addition to the auctioneer's fee of up to 10% of the sale price. Many bidders bring their enclosed trucks or trailers to reduce transportation costs.

Now, any seller hopes to discover concealed firearms, cash, or gems, but in my experience, persons who have left such excellent items generally have enough money to pay their rent.

Daily, you will find items such as extra furniture, Christmas decorations, clothing, and about everything you will find at a garage sale or flea market. In addition, you should appropriately value things in your offers. Bidders "overbidding" is a typical occurrence, as is the discovery of an exotic Japanese sword or the whole run of The Incredible Hulk comics, etc.

You must also possess a strong stomach. Many individuals utilize their storage spaces as a dump, with items strewn around. The buyer is responsible for sweeping the apartment clean. Do not be surprised to find highly, incredibly intimate objects. We have observed prosthetic limbs, sexual toys, and sufficient "porn" to open an x-rated store.

Our most profitable product is furniture. Not many bidders enjoy the labor required to remove and relocate a whole home's worth of furniture, but I've discovered that furniture is a reliable source of revenue. Next come the electrical items, such as lamps, toasters, and clock radios, appear to sell swiftly. Rarely does anyone leave "genuine" jewelry.

No gold, some silver, and primarily a quartz movement watch. Simply do not overpay. I have not seen a "drug dealer's money box" in any of the storage units I've purchased, but if I had, I wouldn't tell anyone! Happy bidding!

CHAPTER 30

SURVEILLANCE EQUIPMENT

There are many methods to generate a little extra money or a living using CCTV products and monitoring equipment. This can be accomplished in different ways, with varying degrees of complexity, depending on how much effort you are willing to invest.

Become A Dealer / Installer - Difficulty: Requires Advanced Knowledge

If you have a knack for installing active electronics and solid technical knowledge, this could be an excellent way to make a living.

You have to register as a dealer with a surveillance distributor first. By doing so, you will receive access to dealer pricing plans that allow you to purchase CCTV equipment in bulk at a discount. You can then mark up these products and sell them to installers or clients directly if you do not offer installation services.

If you opt to install the equipment, you will also be allowed to collect installation fees.

This can offer a lucrative way to earn money but requires significant effort and study into issues such as installation liability insurance and return and warranty information.

Repurpose Old Surveillance Cameras - Low Experience Required Difficulty

This won't make you rich but can lead to a bit of side business that generates rapid income. You can make money from this by locating old and broken security cameras, cleaning them up, and selling them as dummy cameras to those on tight budgets who want a burglar deterrent lower than they would pay for a fully functional security camera.

To locate these cameras, you can look for failing firms or surveillance installers with dead parts that would otherwise be discarded tomorrow.

Rent Out Cameras and Services - Medium Degree Of Expertise Required

This entails researching on your behalf, but if done correctly, it can result in a respectable supplementary income.

Your first option is to purchase a certain quantity of surveillance equipment and rent it to customers daily or according to any other time and pricing scheme, you deem appropriate. This may necessitate getting a company license and implementing effective policies to secure your equipment from abuse.

You might also try becoming a surveillance monitor in your community. You might install a system that monitors your neighborhood for criminal activities and charge your neighbors for its operation and monitoring. Before acquiring your equipment, you should confirm that this is acceptable to your neighbors.

Finally, you may establish a small firm that specializes in monitoring people's businesses and houses while they are absent. For this to function, the places you are monitoring must have a surveillance system installed, and their feeds must be networked so that you can monitor them from your home monitor setup. You may even offer to install their surveillance network.

CHAPTER 31

FREE CLASSIFIED POSTING SERVICE

You desire a vacation but cannot afford even a day excursion to a local amusement park. If so, look at your home; you may have the funds right under your feet - or at least in a box under your bed or your basement/garage. You may currently refer to it as clutter, but it's unclaimed cash that can be converted through a free classified posting service!

Look around your house. What items do you no longer require? In addition to the garage, basement, and attic, the children's rooms and the kitchen are excellent areas to begin your search.

Here you can find nearly new toys that have been played with only a few times and undesired kitchen appliances that you thought would make your life easier - and perhaps they would have if you had ever used them! Once you have a collection of items that can be repurposed, select a free classified posting service to put them on.

The advantage of a free classified posting service is that it will only require your time. You will not lose valuable bucks on listing prices. You can advertise as many products as you choose without paying listing costs in advance and hope they sell. There is no financial risk for you.

After locating the free ad posting service you choose, you must evaluate each item you intend to list. To prevent dissatisfied customers, you must carefully inspect each item and document any damage. Baby wipes or a soft cloth with regular household soap and water are quick methods to clean anything that requires a little polishing so that it sparkles like new.

If your selected free ad posting service permits photographs, use a digital camera (borrow one if you don't have one) to take shots of each item, including any damaged parts, so potential purchasers can examine them before agreeing to purchase.

Each item's description should include its essential characteristics, condition, special remarks (such as significant damage or limited editions), and price. Examine listings for similar products already posted on the free classified posting service to gain a ballpark estimate of your item's value. You should also specify that the items are "used" and that all sales are final so that you don't end up with returned items.

Now that you've listed the stuff, all that's left to do is wait for the free ad posting service to turn your clutter into cash. This outstanding payment or long-awaited amusement park vacation may be financed sooner than anticipated.

CHAPTER 32

A RENTAL PROPERTY

During this downturn in the real estate market, many owners of second houses confront a problem. Does reducing the family's budget necessitate the sale of this needless luxury? Perhaps not necessarily.

By converting the second house into a holiday rental, families can generate income and, in most situations, retain the property. In addition, unlike long-term rentals, holiday rentals allow the family to continue living in the home between bookings.

Many families have loved their second houses for decades or even generations. Converting your property into a holiday rental can be a sensible decision. Since the second house is already furnished, the changeover requires minor adjustments.

Even typically, long-term rental properties can be decorated and modified. Staging helpers with specialized training can assist in this area. During the "high season," weekly rental rates are often equivalent to the regular monthly rental rate, making it simple to cover the increased expenses.

Despite the recession, vacation rentals have continued to increase in popularity. Families requiring many rooms can save money by renting a home rather than staying in a standard hotel.

Surprisingly, many guests report that the most significant appeal of the home is the opportunity to experience the community atmosphere and local flavor, which can be lacking in hotels located in tourist hubs.

So how do we begin? Many DIY websites allow property owners to list their rental properties. Owners simply submit photographs, a description, and rental pricing. Availability is monitored using an integrated calendar function.

Some owners use a full-service real estate agent who specializes in holiday rentals. You can receive support with some services, ranging from handling queries and bookings to managing the cleaning team, for a percentage of the rental fee.

CHAPTER 33

USED AUTOMOBILES!

A car is one of the most significant purchases individuals make. The typical consumer acquires a new automobile every few years. Due to the high price of new vehicles, millions of individuals purchase affordable used cars.

There are colossal opportunities to generate a superb income. Help meet the massive demand for affordable secondhand cars of excellent quality. When starting, you should concentrate on automobiles priced under $4,000.

Conduct research to determine which automobiles are the most popular and best-selling in your area. By remaining in the lower price ranges with these popular automobiles, you will be in a higher-demand market. More people can afford them than higher-priced, more expensive cars, making it much easier to profit rapidly.

This is a crucial aspect of your success: you earn money by purchasing. You must pay the wholesale price or less minus the cost of any necessary repairs and other charges, such as detailing, newspaper advertisements, etc.

After learning the wholesale price, fewer repair fees, and other expenses, you will know what you can spend on a car. If you buy it correctly, you can sell it for a profit while still offering an outstanding value to the buyer.

Among the most significant things you can do to buy a used car at a discount is to conduct research. Check the local classified advertisements to get the asking price for the type of vehicle you're interested in purchasing.

Here are a few fantastic sites for pricing information:

NADA GUIDES - [http://www.nadaguides .com]

KELLEY BLUE BOOK - http://www.kbb.com

EDMUNDS - http://www.edmunds.com

CARFAX is an additional resource to review. They can provide you with a vehicle history report. The National Highway Traffic Safety Administration includes a section for researching the recall history of automobiles. We recommend that your mechanic evaluate the vehicle you are interested in purchasing before making the purchase.

Newspaper Classified Ads are a great way to find cars priced much below retail. Many of these individuals will gladly sell their used cars for many hundred dollars more than what the dealer charged, resulting in an EXCEPTIONAL DEAL!

Online auctions can be an excellent location to discover deals. You can shop from the convenience of your home. Look for auctions without a reserve; these auctions do not have a minimum selling price.

Public Automobile Auctions are accessible to the general public and do not require a Dealer's License. Public auctions are an ideal venue for acquiring automobiles at wholesale pricing. These auctions include Credit Union, Bank, and Lending Institution Repossessions. Some public auctions also sell autos owned by the police, local municipalities, cities, states, and counties.

Estate and Bankruptcy Auctions might be a great place to purchase wholesale automobiles. These auctions are typically publicized in the classified section of newspapers or managed by Probate Estate Auctioneers.

Government auctions are a great source of inexpensive automobiles. They include vehicles from the FBI, the Internal Revenue Service, DEA drug raid seizures, U.S. Customs Auctions, the Department of Defense, General Services Auctions, the Resolution Trust Corporation, the United States

Postal Service, and the Department of Housing and Urban Development.

Often, rental car companies auction off their fleets. They are a significant source of automobiles. Contact these huge companies for more information.

Dealer Auctions might be one of the finest places to find vehicles at costs below wholesale. Most of these auctions require a dealer's license. These auctions include fleet automobiles, lease autos, trade-ins, and rentals.

Avoid purchasing old vehicles that require extensive mechanical or body repairs. If the vehicle paint is a bit dull or the carpet is dirty, you can detail, polish, wax the automobile, and clean the carpet. As needed, replace the floor mats.

A few hours of repair can increase the value of your vehicle by hundreds or even thousands of dollars. By maintaining a clean exterior and interior, you will attract more buyers who are eager to pay top prices for your vehicle.

When your car is fit to be sold, you can publish an ad in the classified section of your local newspaper, or you can use the internet to reach a larger audience. CARS.COM and AUTOBYTEL.COM get a lot of traffic and are costly.

Online auctions for the sale of automobiles have also grown in popularity. It has become one of the simplest, quickest, and most cost-effective ways to reach hundreds or even thousands of people who are interested in your car. Both EBAYMOTORS.COM and AUCTIONYOURAUTOS.COM are auction websites.

Most states require a dealer's license to purchase and sell vehicles for profit. For further information on how to get a dealer's license, consult your state's Department of Motor Vehicles or Department of Public Safety. Consult your attorney, insurance agent, accountant, and other government officials to determine what permits, licenses, records, insurance policies, etc., are necessary.

CHAPTER 34

DELIVERING GROCERIES

F amilies are getting busier and busier. Since days begin at the crack of dawn and end in a whirlwind of activity, many household errands are sometimes neglected. After school, work, sports, and other commitments, grocery shopping is the last thing a busy parent wants to do.

Suppose you are a self-motivated individual looking for a business that is simple to operate, low-cost, and flexible. In that case, a grocery delivery service may be the ideal way to earn money. You can amass a large clientele within a few weeks with an essential website, fliers, and word-of-mouth marketing.

You can start earning money by basing your fee structure on a flat rate up to a specific percentage of the entire shopping spend. For instance, 10% of a food bill of $125.00 would be $12.50, or you can charge a flat fee of $15.00 up to a grocery expenditure of $150.00. If you need to visit multiple stores, you can add additional costs. If a consumer wishes to use coupons, you may charge a small fee to get them before the trip.

Many grocery retailers now maintain online shopping lists. If a store does not have one, you may be able to get one by outlining the services your organization provides. This is a win-win situation for the company and you, as you can list their products for the convenience of your consumers. The store may receive additional business from customers who would not usually visit their location.

In addition, you may wish to collaborate with coupon websites to get the best deals for your customers while also generating additional revenue for the coupon websites. You can profit as your clients save money.

This service is a boon for clients who lack a vehicle, are disabled, elderly, recovering from illness or accident, or are simply too busy to drive themselves. Also, you may offer to collect other items, such as dry cleaning or medicines. Though there may be short-term circumstances in which your skills are required, it would be great to develop a basis for recurring customers.

The schedule flexibility of this type of business is another advantage of ownership. You can determine your working hours and days. You may also be able to request longer hours on days following the release of circulars and coupons, often on Tuesdays and Sundays. It is possible to work as few or as many hours and days as desired in this form of business.

You can earn money delivering groceries if you have business knowledge, a car, and a desire to be your boss while still helping people. Your business can be operational within a week if you have a solid business plan and affordable start-up expenses.

Consider all the busy folks you know and multiply their number by ten bucks. Then, consider how many active people they know, double that number by 10 dollars, and you can see how it can earn money delivering groceries.

CHAPTER 35

VEHICLE ADVERTISING

Over two million individuals profit from advertising on their vehicles. A typical billboard automobile can provide a monthly income of up to $600. Every year, businesses invest countless billions of dollars in marketing and advertising. If you have an impressive driving record and an excellent vehicle and drive more than 1,000 miles per month, you can make money by displaying advertisements on your car.

The automobile wrap is a means of making money through advertising. This is where your car gets surrounded by adverts. Many of them were designed by professionals. You have an option of what you will or will not let be promoted on your automobile, but if you turn down one firm, it may be quite some time before you are accepted for another advertisement. Often, you cannot pick how your vehicle is wrapped. This advertising cannot be eliminated.

If you have moral concerns about the marketing you give, keep this in mind. Remember that this aims to promote the company's products or services. They desire extensive exposure. Some companies use in-car GPS trackers to track the number of miles driven. You may also be required to bring the vehicle for advertisement durability inspections.

A second method of making money with mobile billboards involves advertising companies providing individuals with wrapped vehicles and allowing them to drive them for free. The average vehicle lifespan is between two and five years.

This program provides an accessible vehicle to drive, but you are not compensated for the monthly commercials.

Typically, the only costs associated with this scheme for the motorist are insurance and gasoline.

Before enrolling in an automobile advertising program, you must satisfy the following requirements:

- The minimum age is eighteen years old.
- You must have a valid driver's license
- You must have a clean vehicle.
- You must have an excellent driving record

Once accepted into a car advertising program, you must sign an agreement stipulating the daily distance you drive, the daily period you go, and the daily driving hours. Your partnership with the advertising firm may be canceled if you misrepresent this information and the company discovers it.

These automobile advertising programs are in high demand among motorists. You might search "get paid to drive" or "vehicle advertising" to locate a company that provides these services. Accessing the advertiser's directory on many websites requires filling out an application and paying a one-time fee. This cost is typically less than fifty bucks.

Typically, a trustworthy business will not charge additional expenses for the service. Check out car advertising if you have an outstanding driving record, drive many hours daily, and want to make money.

CHAPTER 36

PEDICURE EQUIPMENT

Many individuals ignore their feet and desire a pedicure but may not know where to get one. You can now provide this service in your region. Equipment for pedicures might aid in the expansion of a salon's company. This enables you to acquire additional business from your existing and new consumers.

People enjoy spoiling themselves, and what better way to make a day memorable than by receiving the whole salon treatment? Investing in pedicure equipment could dramatically increase your earning margins. It may be less expensive than you anticipate to add the necessary components to offer this service.

Some chairs can be used as regular chairs and converted to pedicure chairs when necessary. This can be an excellent space saver for smaller salons. Chairs for pedicures include a basin for cleaning the feet and space for storing additional equipment.

Lotions are an absolute necessity for pedicures. These can assist in smoothing rough skin and softening the foot. This procedure may also assist customers in relaxing while their feet are massaged. You may require scrapers to remove dead skin.

For nails, clippers and filers are often required. While many women enjoy manicuring nails, many dread doing it themselves. If you already offer manicures, it is likely that you already have a good portion of the equipment necessary to add pedicures to your list of services. Toenail clippers may need to be larger than those used for manicures.

Check out the available pedicure equipment for your salon today. Do not risk losing business because you do not provide what your clients desire. Used equipment may be open, and a business license enables wholesale purchases.

CHAPTER 37

PROFITABLE PC REPAIRS

It is believed that at least two-thirds of U.S. households have at least one computer, which is expanding each year exponentially. Among the exciting things about this is that you may earn an excellent income even if you have just rudimentary computer skills.

I've been operating a little computer repair business out of our home for years; it's a simple way to make money without investing any capital, as most of your services will be for labor only.

I discovered that a computer programming or engineering degree is not required to fix common computer problems. Due to not paying attention to what they are doing or where they are going on the Internet, many of today's issues are generated by pop-ups and malware.

If you can back up files, run antivirus software such as Norton Antivirus and install and run adware software, you can earn substantial money with no effort.

This is merely the tip of the iceberg, but at least in my experience, it is one of the most often recurrent issues encountered by home computer users. I make repeated journeys to individuals' houses for the same issues. Most of our computer repair company comprises repeat business from satisfied clients, which I don't mind.

As long as you offer a fair fee for your work, you will be rehired; also, nothing is better than a delighted customer to provide you with an abundance of referrals.

The reformat is one of my favorites, for which we charge a fixed cost; many fear this easy aspect of computer maintenance. Therefore I perform dozens of them. Nothing is better than being compensated well for sitting around and occasionally pressing a few keys.

I discovered that minor format changes and other basic upkeep led to a need for upgrades, which is where the real money is produced. I purchase the components from a discount warehouse and resell them at retail, plus the expense of installing them and their software.

While I have the case open, I can recommend a cleaning, as there is likely dust within. Since cleaning should be performed routinely, this also results in greater repeat business. Soon, you will have a stable income based solely on your talents, which will only increase, like the number of computers in households.

Try what I did if you need money immediately or within the hour. I am making more money today than I did in my previous business, and you can, too, if you click the link below and read the incredible accurate tale. I was suspicious for only ten seconds after joining before I knew what this was. You will also be beaming from ear to ear, as I was. Imagine tripling your money each week with negligible or no risk!

CHAPTER 38

MLM PROGRAMS

MLM (multi-level marketing) programs are one of the best methods to make money on the Internet, and the MLM sector is one of the largest in the world, generating hundreds of millions of dollars per month. Successful in this industry might earn thousands of dollars per month.

After joining the program and paying the membership fee, you will receive access to the items, promotional materials, websites, training videos, and customer service.

MLM programs sell different items and services, including periodicals, books, cleaning supplies, and pet food. The concept is to utilize the product yourself, sell a certain number of goods each month, and recruit others to do the same.

The most challenging phase is recruiting people to join the program under your line. Many Internet marketing and advertising strategies can recruit people for your downline, including free classified posting, email marketing, pay-per-click (PPC), article marketing, banner advertising, and pop-ups.

There are thousands of MLM programs available. Before creating an account with one of them, you should examine their compensation programs, the products they sell, and Google to see if there are any scam complaints about the program.

Recruiting as many referrals as possible is the most critical aspect of developing a successful MLM business; without them, it would be tough to earn money.

CHAPTER 39

EBAY

There are virtually no individuals in the modern world who are unfamiliar with eBay. Consequently, this may be the solution if you want a simple approach to making money.

One of the primary reasons eBay has grown so popular is the variety of available things. You can find virtually anything on eBay, from your next apparel purchase to a sought-after work of art and even a strand of celebrity hair.

Although eBay buying is enjoyable, why stop there? There are also many options for you to begin earning money on eBay. Thankfully, it is not a challenging task, and virtually anyone would be capable of performing it.

Choosing what you will sell is the first step in selling something. You can sell anything, so be creative and consider your target demographic and the market carefully. Since different people are trying to purchase other products on eBay, even an item that seems useless to your family could end up being the most lucrative on eBay.

So remember that what you consider meaningless may be a treasure to someone else. Therefore, one straightforward approach to making money on eBay is sorting through your old belongings, cleaning out your garage, closets, and basement, and getting ready to make money.

One thing to remember to be confident and respectful is to weigh items and set an accurate delivery charge. Also, be prompt in mailing products that have been sold; do not delay. Remember that when you have an online selling business, all potential buyers have to go on is your seller rating, so work diligently to keep a high rating. Keeping in mind the contentment of your customers will be of great assistance to you.

This is especially crucial when dealing with eBay, as they work hard to assure excellent customer service and the absence of dishonest vendors and purchasers. Remember that the more seller points you have, the more products you can sell. Ensure that you work diligently on each sale you make.

CHAPTER 40

PRODUCE CLEANING PRODUCTS

Nowadays, cleaning products are available in a vast array of varieties. Unfortunately, most of them are chemical-based and, as a result, introduce toxic compounds into our homes. The worst thing is that you must pay high costs for these potentially dangerous products.

Do not be easily duped by cleaning products that have a pleasant odor or claim to contain a single natural component. Many corporations make similar promises to conceal the fact that their products contain unpleasant substances.

So why not simply create your cleaning supplies? This is the ideal answer, as it will give you peace of mind that your family won't be exposed to dangerous chemicals and will also help you save money. Also, utilizing natural cleaning products is an environmentally responsible option.

You need only a few essential cleaning materials to create your cleaning products. These are well-known, including lemon, vinegar, and baking soda.

As a result of its inherent antiseptic characteristics, vinegar is the most extensively touted natural cleaner for the house. It is a multipurpose cleaner that may be used on nearly all surfaces, excluding marble. It is also highly effective at eliminating offensive odors. In addition, although vinegar has a sour smell, it eventually vanishes after it dries.

To aid in reducing the odor, dilute the vinegar with water. Vinegar can also be used as a less expensive alternative to fabric softeners, and it can remove the unsightly rings that form on the rim of your toilet bowl. Also, vinegar is particularly excellent in cleaning glass and mirrors.

In contrast, lemon contains inherent antibacterial and antiseptic qualities. It helps remove stains from textiles and sanitize kitchen drains. Due to its firm acidity, it also functions as a natural bleaching agent. Also, lemon is excellent for eliminating hardened soap scum or hard water minerals from sinks and cleaning any brass or copper household fixtures.

Lastly, baking soda might also be used. Due to its abrasive characteristics, this is one of the most powerful natural cleaners in removing grime, grease, and mildew. In addition, it is an excellent deodorizer.

Due to its capacity to remove grime, discoloration, and odor, many households use baking soda to clean bathtubs and refrigerators. In fact, by just placing a package of baking soda in your refrigerator, it will absorb offensive scents. Also, it can be used to clean and remove rust from ovens and polish metals.

These three ingredients can be used to clean your home without exposing your family to dangerous substances. Once you learn what each of these chemicals is capable of, you can combine them to create your cleaning products.

CHAPTER 41

PROVIDING LAUNDRY AND IRONING SERVICES

Whether it be school, work or family, most people today are too busy to iron and wash their clothes (unless they want to wear the same clothes repeatedly!). It appears to be an impossible assignment; I wish there were a more straightforward method to complete it. Here is where you are most needed.

Because everyone has filthy clothing, laundry, and ironing dirty clothes is a business, not just a small one but a potentially large one. You might also create a website that lists the price of the service for potential consumers.

This business can be conducted at the customer's house or home if you have a large basement or spare room, allowing you to store the garments without transferring them! You could rent a store or building for this business if finances allow.

Your most significant expenditure would be a washer, dryer, and iron. Aside from the customer service desk in front of the area, the rest of the space does not require expensive repairs. You essentially need a lot of space.

Hiring temporary or permanent personnel is beneficial, depending on the speed of your job and the volume of laundry you wish to process. This is a fantastic family business where everyone joins in, or if you are a student in need of spending money! It would be similar to washing the family's laundry - a VERY LARGE load, and the cash will accompany each bucket of soiled clothing.

CHAPTER 42

WEB VIDEOS

There are numerous ways to make money online; some are very enjoyable. This section examines two odd ways to earn money from web videos. People are adopting different methods to earn money online, and you can too.

Revver.com pays you for every view of your video. Most video sites are geared to profit from advertising. People who visit the website to watch videos may click on advertisements from Google AdSense or another advertising service.

Many service-providing websites generate revenue through advertising, and the proprietors keep all of it. The rationale is that they use the funds to provide free access to the site's services.

Not true of Revver.com. This website will share revenue generated from advertisements associated with your video with the creator. The website features a dynamic advertising system that displays advertisements based on the content of the video and awards a portion of the earnings to your account.

Therefore, it is feasible to earn money by submitting high-quality films and getting compensated when interested parties see the linked advertisements. You can embed a video from Revver.com on your site and receive payment each time it is seen, and an ad is clicked. The wider your videos' distribution, the greater your earnings.

A second approach to earning money from videos is to host them on your website and receive payment for each view. The Voxant NewsRoom program's specifications are available at thenewsroom.com. You are compensated on a CPM basis each time someone watches your video and earns money.

Making money on thenewsroom.com is not tricky. Simply create an account and conduct a keyword search to browse the available videos. Post the movies to your website or blog and begin to get income. Merely follow the site's instructions, which provide step-by-step directions on embedding any video on your website.

The technique operates by generating a one-of-a-kind code that you embed in a website of your choosing. You make money on autopilot each time the video is seen without selling anything.

These are two additional methods for generating revenue on thenewsroom.com. You can post select articles on your website and be compensated each time the content is accessed, and the associated advertisement is displayed. You can make money by recommending individuals to Newsroom.

We live in the age of information. Those with the proper knowledge will be compensated, especially online, where chances are limitless. Revver and Newsroom's moneymaking opportunities are home-based residual income because they earn revenue for many days after initial setup.

CHAPTER 43

SURVEYS

According to experts, 38% of researchers and businesses devote time and resources to online marketing research, which is not unexpected.

It is one technique to gain access to a broad market where demographics, lifestyle, and other factors simplify classifying individuals. Due to the existence of this industry, it is a perfect method to begin working from the convenience of your home.

People who like to work from home can access many opportunities on the web market. Many websites provide different money-making options. Paid online surveys are one of the web industry's most effective services. People weary of going to work turn to money-making activities such as surveys. When you Google "online market survey possibilities," about six million results are returned.

Many individuals participate in paid surveys. Millions are doing it presently, and now, you may effortlessly begin earning money by completing surveys. The following are three simple steps for making money through online surveys.

Finding survey businesses accepting new panelists is the first step in earning money through service. Search engines are a valuable resource for locating these businesses. If you use search terms such as "online paid surveys," you'll likely find many suitable possibilities.

The companies for which you should work are those with a solid reputation for paying for internet surveys. Popular online survey sites include Synovate, American Consumer Opinion, Survey Spot, Sendearnings, and many others.

With these companies, you can earn money, and the surveys may even interest you. The average salary range for each survey is $3 to $5. Always remember that not all these surveys pay money for your participation. However, completing more surveys increases your likelihood of receiving payment.

The next step in earning money through surveys is to keep an eye out for emails issued by the company for whom you work. Every two weeks, the company will send you an email requesting you to participate in their surveys.

When you identify a website for which you would like to work, you log in and complete the survey. Typically, the initial questions are demographic selectors, such as age, gender, typical household income, household size, etc. When you respond to these questions, they will be categorized based on your responses.

The surveys you may be asked to complete about items or specific purchasing habits. When you qualify, you will be allowed to continue the study. It typically takes approximately 10 minutes and includes questions about your spending and purchasing patterns.

The final step is to finish the survey. They are straightforward and need no effort to complete. The average amount of time required to complete the survey is 15 minutes. The income and frequency may vary depending on the website for which you work.

CHAPTER 44

WEB HOSTING

The timing is ideal to discover how to earn money with web hosting. To put it lightly, many people have made a lot of money using the Internet. These facts have not gone unnoticed, as many individuals and businesses have realized many opportunities to earn money online.

Creating one's website is possible, but a dependable hosting service is unquestionably preferable. Creating your services provides far more opportunities to earn a substantial income and is a viable solution.

Web services is a substantial industry, but fortunately, there is ample potential for new entrants. Most persons who have made a living supplying web services have amassed significant wealth. Reseller web hosting is a good option if you are just starting to offer web services.

To be successful with online services, it is vital to supply massive storage and bandwidth. Therefore, you should investigate the unlimited avenues, as they are ideal for individuals seeking online services with total space, bandwidth, and email accounts.

If you want to make money from delivering web services, customer satisfaction is an additional issue that must be addressed. In reality, offering your customers dependable and quick hosting at a low price is essential.

In addition, you must actively discover how to attract more potential customers to your hosting website. You must design effective marketing techniques and have a good internet presence. In other words, you must be easily discoverable when customers use a search engine to locate hosting services.

By providing outstanding hosting services, you can earn money online. In this regard, consider the possibility of article marketing, blogs, and text link ads, all of which can assist in attracting a large number of people to your hosting site. Engaging a consultant who can show you how to market your website is also beneficial. However, you may find the same information by utilizing a search engine.

Using the major search engines to determine what other online services are doing and how they got started is one strategy to monetize your hosting website. Next, determine where they are and what their primary business goals are. Simultaneously, you should be well aware of your business goals, which should be checked periodically to ensure that you are on the right track.

Reseller hosting is an excellent method for generating revenue from your web hosting services. In this hosting, you must purchase a hosting plan that you can resell for a profit. Web admins have long been aware of this method for making money on the Internet. The good news is that reseller hosting plans are inexpensive to acquire.

You can acquire sufficient area to generate a profit by investing approximately thirty dollars per month. Few individuals are willing to invest $1,000 to get a dedicated server. Reseller hosting is highly effective in generating revenue from your web hosting services. It is simple to learn how to make money with web hosting. With available solutions such as reseller services, nothing could be simpler.

CHAPTER 45

SECRETARIAL SERVICE

Creating your secretarial service may be the answer if you have excellent typing abilities and seek a means to make money without spending.

As the economy deteriorates, many companies are searching for cost-cutting measures while still requiring the services of a professional secretary. You will be excited by the number of local businesses that would welcome assistance with their paperwork and day-to-day operations.

If you want to get work and make a living, the secretarial service of today should be prepared to provide different services. Some of these services are the same as those performed by secretaries for years, such as typing other papers, generating bills for customers, and handling the mail.

However, the modern secretary can also handle the company website, track company spending using spreadsheets, and execute data entry jobs using their computer.

In addition, you should be prepared to answer directed phone calls, plan workplace events and give your employer some level of customer service. All of this can be achieved from the comfort of your own home. With a little effort and solid organizational abilities, you will soon be working for multiple clients simultaneously.

You presumably already own the only necessary equipment, including a computer, a printer, and a telephone, so there is no cost related to getting started. Other than this, the only things you need to give an excellent service are your knowledge and commitment to working hard.

Among the simplest ways to find a job is to print a flyer that clearly defines the services you want to offer using your computer talents. You should list any special training, such as your proficiency with Excel, MS Word, Lotus, and other software. You may want to place a prominent offer in the middle of your flyer that gives potential new clients a discount for trying your services.

Take these flyers to every business in town and offer your services to the office manager or business owner. If they respond that they do not require assistance at this time, offer to assist them with future overflow work and leave them with your flyer and business cards. A "no" today could be a "yes" tomorrow, so do not be afraid to check in with all these firms frequently.

It takes time to create a business, but with perseverance, you will soon have an excellent secretarial service that has allowed you to earn money without requiring a substantial investment.

CHAPTER 46

OFFLINE BUSINESS CONSULTING

Offline business consulting has generated widespread interest among internet marketers. Those with a few years of expertise in Internet marketing can profit from taking their business offline.

It has been demonstrated that starting an internet consulting business with offline clients generates more money than exposing yourself to the public as an online freelancer, even though some of its claims look hype. Before discussing how to make money online with this new venture, let's define offline business counseling.

Many offline, brick-and-mortar businesses also use the Internet to sell their services. The issue with these firms is that they are so focused on their services that they likely have no idea how to promote their company online. An experienced internet marketer can serve as a professional internet company adviser at this point.

Here are a few suggestions for services you can provide offline businesses that are certain to increase your income:

Web design and SEO (Search Engine Optimization)

Having an internet presence is a newfound experience for some of these firms. Offering to create their website can make a substantial income. This service could become your specialty if you have been establishing and maintaining your website. You can also offer on-site optimization or SEO as part of the service. Again, if you are a professional internet marketer, SEO is the area in which you are an expert.

Establish a blog for the company.

Other firms may already have static websites that were developed specifically for them. If you ask the business owners if they have made money from their websites, they will likely express dismay that the website has not generated as many sales as they had hoped.

By proposing to develop a blog for their firm, you may earn up to $500 for each organization. Customers should be able to communicate with the firm via the blog, and the company should use the blog to inform customers of new items and promotions.

Utilizing many social media to launch their campaigns

For a business to expand, it must utilize social networking platforms like Facebook, Twitter, LinkedIn, MySpace, and Plaxo. These sites might provide them with access to prospective customers in their regions. Even if you are just starting to use social media, you can give this as one of your services.

The service entails creating a profile on all social media platforms and linking them to Friendfeed, where customers can manage all their social networks from one location. You may still quickly charge up to $500.00 for this service just to establish their profiles on all these social networks.

If you're ready to go the extra mile, you can also offer to maintain these services for a monthly cost, thereby increasing your income. Here is how to make money through offline business counseling on the Internet.

CHAPTER 47

ARTICLE MARKETING SERVICES

If you aim to earn money through article marketing, there are some article marketing firms accessible to assist you. However, generating articles and submitting them to article directories, the essence of article marketing, will not generate income; you also need a product and a website.

This essay is not about items or websites; I'm merely pointing out that article marketing services do not generate revenue on their own. It is an internet marketing strategy that will deliver visitors to your web pages, after which it is up to you to generate revenue.

Having said that, how do you make money with article marketing services? The following article's marketing strategies should assist you in profiting from the products or services you offer by giving a free and effective web promotion. This is an uncommon mix today when the term "free" on the Internet often means outmoded!

The Goal of the article Marketing

The goal of article marketing is to convince readers of your content to visit your website by clicking on the link. That's all! It is not to persuade them to acquire something or to be especially interested in your goods; instead, it encourages them to click on the URL provided in your resource or byline.

If you opt to use online article marketing services, they can help you get that click, but they don't have anything to do with the money you can earn from that click. So let's say that your landing page, which is included in the 'author's re-sources' portion of your post, is well-designed and persua-sive enough to convince them to purchase your product or service.

Here are the steps required to bring them there:

The article's Title and Abstract

The title and summary are pretty vital. These will attract the attention of potential clients. This title can exist in three locations:

a) Regarding the article directory: your articles will be submitted to article directories, which will publish them with the title and synopsis you specify. The headline will attract a potential reader who will read the summary. If the synopsis compels the reader to read the article, you have completed the initial step.

b) On a reader's website: Generally, readers are entitled to copy your article and use it as material on any web pages related to the theme of your post. This can be a significant boost for your article and as more of your articles are published on other websites, making money through article marketing becomes much more straight-forward. You get backlinks and reads from these web-sites, which can lead to clicks.

c) On Google: Google receives more than 80 percent of searches on any search engine. Your summary will dis-play on Google as the description (or a portion of the de-scription), and your title will appear as the listing's title.

If you have chosen the right keyword and written the arti-cle correctly with good LSI conformance, you have a better chance of being ranked on Google's Page 1 with all the traffic that brings. Making money using article marketing services suddenly becomes simpler!

The article's Text

Writing articles is a skill few possess; therefore, article writing and article marketing services are required to get good rankings for your content. You do not need your website to be mentioned if your articles are featured, as the byline of each piece has a link to your website. You can present any URL in your resource, sometimes two or three.

The article Reference

This is what we've been discussing throughout the entirety of this post. This is the essence of making money with article marketing services: the "author's resource" you use to convince readers that you can fix their problem if they click the link. If you know what you're doing, providing two or three links gives them a selection, which may be pretty effective. If not, you will fail by providing multiple options.

By utilizing professional article marketing services, you can be confident that each of these aspects of your article is written correctly and with the appropriate amount of emphasis, without violating directory terms and conditions or Authors' Guidelines and that your article will provide you with the most significant opportunity to earn money through article marketing.

CHAPTER 48

PEER MONEY LENDING SERVICES

D ue to the financial crisis, it has become increasingly difficult for individuals to borrow money at a reasonable interest rate. Banks and credit card businesses have implemented stringent lending policies and procedures. Consumers are now confronted with the difficulty of rising interest rates. Under these conditions, consumers are turning to peer-to-peer lending organizations for personal loans.

These businesses can provide lower interest rates and fees than traditional banks and credit card firms. While most people use peer-to-peer lending services to borrow money, did you know that some individuals make money using these services?

To earn money through peer-to-peer lending, you must first register as a lender with a company that provides these services. Prosper and LendingClub are two of the most well-known peer-to-peer lenders. To become a lender, each company has its own set of requirements; individuals should research this information carefully before signing up to lend money.

Assuming you have examined the information and are comfortable with the associated risks, you may now submit loan offers. Before lending money to individuals, you must familiarize yourself with the appropriate procedures.

Principally, peer lenders gain income by lending their funds in exchange for a higher interest rate. The borrower agrees to make monthly principal and interest payments for three years, such as three.

For investors unfamiliar with peer-to-peer lending, this may appear dangerous. What if, after all, the borrower defaults? In this worst-case situation, however, the peer lender loses the amount lent to the borrower.

Given the unpredictability and hazards associated with peer-to-peer lending, what techniques do investors employ to safeguard their capital? First, peer lenders diversify their investments and distribute them among many loans instead of investing everything in a single loan.

Also, astute investors examine the borrower's profile, favoring job stability and avoiding those with a limited work history or a high debt-to-income ratio. Finally, peer lenders reinvest the received interest and principal to capitalize on compound interest.

That concludes the discussion. Peer lenders are developing methods to earn more than the simple interest that conventional banks pay on deposit accounts. While peer-to-peer lending entails greater risk, investors employ different ways to achieve high returns and mitigate risk.

As with any investment, the key is to learn how these services function and how money is earned. Ask experienced investors many questions and begin with a small investment.

CHAPTER 49

HOSTING RESELLER

If you have spent a reasonable time on the Internet over the past years, you have most likely heard of web hosting services. Perhaps some of you have even considered purchasing web hosting space to hold your material and therefore staking your claim on a little portion of cyberspace.

Web hosts are, of course, one of the primary reasons for the existence of the Internet. Without them to host any information you desire, the Internet as we know it today would look drastically different and may not exist at all.

However, many individuals do not realize that you can earn money by becoming an affiliate of a firm that offers reseller hosting. To learn how to accomplish this, let's return to our discussion of web hosts.

Web hosting firms operate solely to provide a service that offers space on their servers to individuals who want to host their material. However, many organizations have gone beyond this service and now offer their customers the ability to act as web hosts independently.

They accomplish this by giving space on their servers to consumers, who then resell this space to their customers. As long as the end user is concerned, they only interact with the purchase of the web space, and the original host is essentially absent.

Depending on the configuration of the secondary server and its agreement with the parent host, there may be no or little evidence that the secondary site is connected to the primary web host. Why do individuals do this, and who is the target market for reseller hosting?

A person may seek to offer hosting services to various consumers as a standalone service or in conjunction with some of his other products. A graphic designer, for instance, may work on a website design project for a client and decide that he might as well offer hosting services to generate additional revenue from what was previously a straightforward design project.

There are, of course, many additional reasons for wishing to offer hosting without actually investing in all the personnel and equipment required to be a full-fledged web host.

Taking advantage of reseller hosting programs that a web host may offer is an additional method of earning money through an affiliation with them. This entails only encouraging others, such as friends or acquaintances, to sign up with the hosting firm. Many companies offer such arrangements, which can be highly beneficial for your organization.

CHAPTER 50

AUTORESPONDERS

The simplest method to generate money with autoresponders is to locate someone ready to pay you a considerable amount to create a series of automatic emails for their prospects and customers.

That isn't easy to accomplish online. Every online marketer realizes the importance of employing an email autoresponder service like Aweber to earn money in today's industry.

Successful Internet marketers know that "the money is on the list."

However, there is a cash-rich market offline that would be happy to pay you incredibly well if you simply approached them.

The best part is that you may reach this market for free. In reality, you likely pass on some of your greatest prospects every day.

I am discussing small business entrepreneurs.

Consider the matter carefully. Most small business owners do not attempt to collect the contact information of prospects and customers who enter their establishments daily.

They are missing out on an enormous fortune. If they followed up with the highly targeted leads and paying customers, they would interact daily, and the profit potential would be immense.

However, most brick-and-mortar small company owners do not know how to follow up with leads and customers.

They do not know how to employ reports, audio, video, and information to pre-educate and convince prospects to purchase their products.

And they don't know how to give back-end products and services to their paying customers to boost income and profits from the advertising and marketing expenditure they've already spent to acquire those customers.

They do not even understand an autoresponder, much less how to make money with one.

Therein is your role.

You can design a straightforward method for collecting the contact information of prospects and clients that enter a small business's location (something like a highly targeted prize that requires people to enter their phone contact details so you can inform them when they win works very well).

Then, you may have the business's staff manually add names, email addresses, and other contact information to the autoresponder list you created specifically for that business.

You also construct follow-up emails with specialized offers for prospects, back-end offers for clients, and relevant content to maintain their interest in receiving your emails.

You can also establish email autoresponder lists designed to follow up with clients after they have purchased or utilized a service.

This could contain instructions on how to use the product, an explanation of what to expect, and suggestions for additional products and services your customers should purchase to improve their experience.

Now, I want you to consider the following.

In most small enterprises, between 50 and 1,000 customers enter their premises daily.

If you were to acquire the contact information of just 20% of these highly focused prospects, you would add between 10 and 200 prospects daily to your email list.

Or 70 to 1,400 a week or an incredible 300 to 6,000 highly targeted leads every month.

I mean it when I say they are highly targeted.

These individuals were sufficiently motivated to leave their houses and drive, walk, cycle or utilize public transportation to visit a business. They have chosen to enter the building for business.

These are wealthy individuals.

And they will spend that money if you present them with an attractive deal.

Do you believe that if you offered to assist a small business owner in converting this incredibly lucrative gold mine of prospects and clients into actual sales and profits utilizing an autoresponder, he would be a tiny bit interested in employing you?

Do you believe he would be willing to pay you to contact thousands of prospects via email regularly if you presented him with the potential purchasing power of such a campaign?

If you collected contact information for three months, your email list would be between 900 and 18,000.

You will generate sales if you send just 1,000 targeted prospects an email containing a well-thought-out offer for a highly focused product or service.

Depending on the quality of the list, you might reasonably anticipate sales between $500 and $2,500.

If you delivered a highly focused offer to 5,000 highly targeted prospects, you could expect to generate between $2,500 and $12,500 in sales.

And you could be sending similar emails each week!

Once you realize how simple it is to generate money by giving this autoresponder service to small business owners for $500 or more per month, you will have no trouble making a profit.

Alternatively, you may charge $1,000 for setting up the autoresponder service and lead collecting system, followed by $250 to $1,000 per month for operating the email follow-up system.

The best part is that you may walk into a business today and leave with a cheque for $500 or more. If you want to earn money with autoresponders, this must be the quickest and most profitable strategy ever invented.

CHAPTER 51

DRIVING A GARBAGE TRUCK

S ince trash is a massive industry, driving a garbage truck can provide a lot of income. At the end of World War II, the growth of the waste management business accelerated. People no longer had the option to burn trash. According to environmental regulations, industrial wastes must be disposed of safely. This section will discuss how you can make money with a garbage truck.

Personal Garbage Collection

The goal of trash collection in urban areas is to ensure that all cities are free of garbage and trash. Metropolitan areas employ garbage trucks for the collection and recycling of industrial waste.

Consequently, garbage truck drivers can sell their services to clean cities. On the other hand, smaller settlements lack the means necessary to purchase cash trucks and employ full-time workers. In certain places, independent operators of garbage trucks can offer their services.

Wasteful Contracts

In large cities, officials contract fleets of garbage trucks for rubbish collection. The majority, however, sign annual contracts with these service providers. You cannot even consider competing with these large companies if you are an independent IT or telecommunications operator.

However, small local entities, such as school districts, are not required to sign long-term agreements. Consequently, you might approach these organizations to offer your services. Since there are many small institutes, you can approach them individually and enter into short-term agreements. This will help you earn a lot of money.

Reusing Waste

You can also get income by providing recycling services. Although local management may have a fleet of garbage vehicles, many cities lack the finances to purchase garbage trucks. Some of them lack sufficient cars for collecting recyclable waste.

As a freelance garbage truck driver, you can gather recyclable waste from many towns and earn a fortune. In addition, you can collect recyclable materials from curbside bins. You can then sell this waste for a substantial profit.

You are responsible for billing and fee collection in this form of firm. Therefore, if you own a garbage truck, this can be a terrific method to make money.

Hazardous Waste Disposal

Corporate trash collection is another lucrative source of revenue for freelancers. This is true in communities that lack access to metropolis services. In other instances, business facilities must engage separate contractors to dispose of their trash.

In addition, you can also offer to collect harmful garbage, such as used motor oil and mercury. This type of waste must be collected and sent to designated recycling locations.

If you own and operate a garbage truck and follow the advice in this section, you can make money. Hopefully, this will assist you in launching a lucrative career as a garbage truck driver.

CHAPTER 52

CAFEPRESS

CafePress has been an online arena for monetizing original design concepts for years. They provide a vast marketplace where anyone may sell designs on various products. However, you will need a few things to get started.

Design Skills & Tools

Although most are known for selling t-shirts, CafePress offers various other customizable products. You may sell your unique artwork on multiple products, including aprons, coffee mugs, clocks, and stickers. But first, you must be able to create original designs!

This does take some design expertise and software. A product featuring visuals and photos will always be more enticing to potential customers, even though it is possible to rely solely on text.

CafePress includes a tool for developing designs that are effective for simple concepts. You may type and edit the text in infinite font sizes, shapes, and colors, select images from a library or upload your photos. This may be all you need to start and make your first sales.

To create genuinely captivating, sales-driving designs, however, you should consider using a third-party, professional-grade graphic design package. Such software can range in price from free (yep, you read it correctly!) to several hundred dollars!

A Touch of Originality

I believe you should be creative to sell designs on CafePress, but I'll say it anyway: You must be creative to sell designs on CafePress!

You must be able to generate concepts that will attract people's attention while they browse the site for items to purchase. In many instances, your designs will be worn on people's bodies! No one will wear a shirt with a boring design, whether it is a graphic image or a simple text one-liner.

Creative concepts that sell well are frequently amusing and inspirational. If you are humorous, you have a lot of work ahead of you!

An Audience

If you intend to sell designs on CafePress, it helps to have a specific audience in mind. You can post designs based on any random concept that comes to mind. Still, if you're targeting a particular niche, you'll have focus, which will help you generate ideas and keep you committed to implementing them.

You probably already have a target audience without even realizing it. What hobbies do you have?

All of these can be targeted using your design concepts. For example, you can create multiple designs for other guitarists if you are a guitarist. You can create humorous drawings with a food theme if you enjoy cooking.

If you persist, making extra money on CafePress can be a fun way to supplement your income. The more designs you upload to CafePress, the greater your earnings potential.

CHAPTER 53

BUSINESS COACHING

Most people do not equate coaching with business because coaching is typically associated with sports training. However, becoming a business coach might be an excellent method to earn additional income. You can even start a genuine home-based business by doing so.

People in business are willing to pay a substantial sum for the assistance of a seasoned professional who can help them achieve success in their field.

The business coach will assist them in maintaining focus and achieving their objectives. These individuals can receive essential help and motivation from a business coach.

Many folks with a respectable home-based business in a subject they are passionate about are now commonplace.

At the top of the list are stay-at-home mothers who need to earn extra money but cannot leave their children with a stranger. They desire to run a successful home-based business but lack the knowledge; here is where you can step in as a business coach.

Many people have fantastic ideas for new or existing products that they would like to sell online or start a respectable home-based business, but they have no idea how to implement them.

You may do them considerably by imparting your business knowledge and guiding them till their firm is prosperous. You will undoubtedly need to be more knowledgeable than your clientele, but you do not need to be an Internet marketing genius in every area.

Anyone operating online is aware that many factors contribute to Internet business success. These include locating a profitable niche, advertising, email list building, marketing, and social networking, to mention a few.

To become a business coach, you will need to concentrate on your area of expertise to establish your niche. Most individuals just starting online are eager to learn from an expert, so this might be an excellent method to earn extra cash.

Initially, it will be prudent to charge slightly less than the usual rate until your customer base has expanded substantially. Everyone is seeking methods to generate extra money. The sooner you begin, the sooner you will have a substantial number of testimonies to support your genuine home-based business.

CONCLUSION

You should have both a short-term and a long-term goal for optimal results. For your short-term goals, you might schedule your week or month. Then, consider where you want your side gig for long-term goals in three or five years. Do you anticipate quitting your job by then? If so, make it one of your long-term goals.

Reward yourself for every significant accomplishment. In any case, it's not easy to run a side business in addition to a full-time job!

Having a side gig and full-time work may leave you exhausted at the end of the day. However, knowing it is doable if you hope to make both careers work. You only need the ability to manage your time.

Whether you like it or not, sacrifices are inevitable. You may need to cut back on some of your favorite weekend activities. Previously, you may have spent your weekends binge-watching Netflix or partying with friends. While you don't need to become a complete bore, you may need to cut back somewhat on enjoyable activities and, you know, focus on adulting and working on your side hustle!

You can do whatever you want with your additional cash. However, if you wish to feel like you're doing something worthwhile with your life, you should save money from your side gig. You might also consider investing in various financial instruments, such as stocks and bonds, to make your money work.

Best wishes!